JOURNEY TO LIFE

Enjoy!

To, Yvonne,

Hasan Kabir

JOURNEY TO LIFE

HASAN P. KABIR

Wesbrook Bay Books
Vancouver, B.C.

Published by Wesbrook Bay Books, Vancouver

www.wesbrookbay.com

Editor: Beverley Boissery

Proofreader:

Book Cover Design: Mitransh Parihar

Interior Design: BDG Sabatini

DEDICATION

Dedicated to

My father Shah Jehan and my mother Ayesha

&

My wife Rasheda,

daughters Shahnaz and Tayna,

their husbands Tahir and Paul,

and grandchildren Zaid and Emad

&

My sister Latifa, her husband Salim and their children Saira, Shazia and Anwar

CONTENTS

Once our daughters Shahnaz and Tanya asked me, "Dad? What was life like when you grew up in Saudi Arabia? How did you reach where you are today?"

The answers are simple, yet complicated. I grew up as a desert boy with no deep roots anywhere but now I have connections everywhere. I grew up as a Muslem But went to Catholic schools in the Sudan, India and Pakistan. I hopped from one school to another as my father's diplomatic postings went. Fresh from Saudi Arabia I switched to a western-style education that landed me in a kindergarten class with six and seven year olds. The problem was that I was eleven. It was embarrassing but I learned that life rewarded dedication, the will to achieve and hard work. My erratic schooling taught me courage and to face every situation with a resolve of steel, and so the desert boy graduated with honors and Bachelor and Master's degrees in geography.

My professional career could not have been better. I started as a senior executive in one of the world's most prestigious oil companies. During the Bangladesh

Liberation War I decided to move my family to West Pakistan and thence back to Jeddah, Saudi Arabia where I had been born. In my childhood it had been a country untouched by outside culture – except, maybe – that of Egypt or the fading Ottoman Empire. I then believed that the whole world was just the walled city of Jeddah, Makkah [Mecca] and Medina. An enigma was beyond the sand dunes. I did not know what rains or lightning were as it rained only once every several years. Then we huddled in a corner, afraid, until it went away. How much I had to learn.

Looking back, I have no regrets.

I have experienced situations far from normal day to day living. I witnessed the Iraqi Revolution in July 1958, the birth of modern India and Pakistan through the partition of the Indian subcontinent, as well as the birth of Bangladesh (formerly East Pakistan) in March 1971. These events opened up vistas previously unknown to me. Perhaps I lived in a world akin to looking through a keyhole with only that view accessible to me. What I had to learn!

This memoir is written from my own perspective. I was brought up in Saudi Arabia, a country where discussion of politics was taboo. My mind was trained not to think and my schooling there was limited to subjects with a religious orientation. Those viewpoints still exist today. I owe a tremendous debt of gratitude to my mother who insisted that her children had to move from Saudi Arabia to get a better education. Had she not fought for us, I most likely would have become a religious educator or a guide to the holy places for pilgrims. The schools I attended in Pakistan and India were as good as those in the United Kingdom or any western institution and they encouraged me to learn and think for myself. I graduated with an honors M.A. degree in Geography, having first achieve my university's medal of distinction for coming first in my B.A./B.Sc. exam. More extraordinary is the fact that I only began "western" schooling when I was eleven and the entire process from Kindergarten to my master's degree took a mere twelve years.

Various political or social views expressed throughout the book were made in informal conversations when Pakistan was splitting into two. I have written about them with no malice, motive, or agenda. March and April of 1971 was a time of life and death for those of us in East Pakistan. Naturally, people said what they thought in their homes or among friends.

My life has been different to the norm. I have seen, heard and been told about strange happenings that are not part of a Canadian world. My stories about the paranormal, the spirit and ghosts were experienced by me or my mother. I believe in the existence of *entities* that live side by side with us. Religious men of most faiths speak of them. There are no convincing proofs. It's a matter of belief. I think maybe *they* feel humans are not yet ready and that exposure may result in social upheaval that may destroy the world order as we know it.

This book is really meant to answer my children's questions. I have included photographs taken by my father and me that captured moments time may have forgotten. But, again, I have no political or other agenda. I am just reporting my view of events and situations that I have lived through. The names of many people are fictitious though they represent actual people.

Hasan Kabir, Vancouver, 2015

CHILDHOOD ENDS

I

I was born in Jeddah, the main port and capital of Saudi Arabia.

Until January 1926 the ancient walled city had been part of the old Ottoman Expire. My mother remembered its conquest by the Saudis and told me stories about it.

The Saudi army had camped outside Jeddah's walls earlier in a siege that lasted for some months, bombarding the city and targeting the Sharif, the ruler's residence a few yards from where she lived. One cannon ball exploded on the wall of a neighbor just opposite a window where my mother's aunt sat.

Splinters penetrated the window, and one lodged into her back. My seven year old mother sat on her lap at the time and was thrown to the floor by the blast of the cannon ball's force.

Days later, after my mother's aunt and uncle had both died. The Sharif left the city and some prominent locals made a deal with the Saudi entourage and opened the city gate.[i] My mother stood on the rooftop of their four storey house and watched the Saud's tribal army rush through the city gate, screaming like a Hollywood version of Red Indians. Some ran aimlessly with their sandals tucked under their armpits, not knowing where to go or what to do. Their leader, Abdul Aziz bin Saud was escorted to one of the homes of the man who had arranged their entrance and the occupation of Jeddah. His family still enjoys the goodwill of the Saudi royalty.

The conquest changed little. The region was still desperately poor with its economy relying on agriculture and money made by pilgrimages to its holy sites and that is where the history of the Kabir family intersects with the area.

My father, Shah Jehan Kabir, was an Indian diplomat and in April 1928 was posted to the British Agency and Consulate at Jeddah (as it was known those days) by the Foreign and Political Department of the Government of India. He was an Indian who knew nothing of the Saudi language or culture. Fortunately, his job as an aide for the Indian pilgrims required neither. I remember when I accompanied him to the port to get into an official sail boat with a well paneled cabin and the British flag flattering on its stern going out to sea to meet a pilgrims ship. Nervous pilgrims negotiated a gangplank on the ship's side and then miraculously managed to hop into the boat.

Shortly after his arrival though, he contracted chicken pox and nervous officials isolated him My father's quarantine lasted several weeks and, when it was over, his belongings were piled up and burnt. My mother, then a fourteen year old, happened to see the tent's yellow flag. "I wonder who that poor man is," she commented to her cousin, totally unaware that in one of life's ironies, the "poor man" would shortly become her husband.

At the time, Jeddah was a few square miles in size with no electricity or piped water. Its narrow roads were dirt and little shops sold vegetables, bread and locally made meals. My father acquired a flat on the second floor of a four storey building that was more than a hundred years old. Its owner, a youth of eighteen, lived above him with his family. The building, along with several others owned by the same young landlord, was in a prime location. A two-storey building housing Chinese diplomats fronted it. To its left was a grand mansion with traditional wooden mesh windows painted red. This had been the official residence of the Sharif of Makkah, the previous ruler of the Hejaz.

My father's building also had the woodworked mesh widows that were so common then in most of the Arab world. Some were painted red, brown or green and the mesh was like a screen so that no one could look in from the outside. Residents inside could see out. Perhaps the mesh windows were for the women to enjoy a view of the outside.

When my father first applied to rent his flat my maternal uncle, eighteen years old at the time, was reluctant to rent it to a man who was not only an Indian but also a bachelor. My father's friends managed to convince him of my father's respectability and, of course, being employed by the British Legation added to his creditability. It took a while longer to win the landlord's trust and the friendship of his sister

and her cousin who was six years old.

Talking didn't work because my father did not know Arabic at that time. So he gifted the family with crates of lemon soda purchased from the ships bringing pilgrims. The younger girl became more and more friendly but her fourteen year old cousin still stood aloof.

Communication was always problematic for my father at first, because his new wife only understood Arabic. Although he struggled with its vocabulary, he generally managed to be understood. But there were mishaps. One morning he asked the house boy to purchase four pieces of vegetables that were long, black and "turban-like" on the top. When he arrived home from the office that afternoon, four Sudanese or Ethiopian males wearing white turbans greeted him. My mother had lined them up on the staircase and locked herself in the apartment when she'd seen them. This was my father's mess to sort out and so she told him. After he'd paid the men, he went upstairs to explain that he'd asked the house boy for four aubergines or eggplants. After that, my Arabic-speaking mother took charge of ordering the groceries.

Not every disaster could be laughed about. They had a child a year later but he died within his first two years. A subsequent child also died, and the third lived for only three years. He was healthy and happy until he suddenly fell ill and also died. My father was completely devastated and so dejected that he contemplated suicide, saying over and over, "My soul, my life, my precious son has gone. I have nothing to live for."

His friends suggested that he live somewhere else because the flat may have been cursed so he called in an old woman to diagnose the problem. Today we would call her a clairvoyant but if she'd been discovered in the Saudi Arabia of the 1930s, she would have been executed. To my father's relief, she came up with an answer. Someone, maybe a sorcerer, had put a spell on the occupants of the house. She couldn't say who did it but after hours of "mumbo-jumbo," she pointed to the entrance of the building.

"There's a spell buried there," she told my anxious parents and asked for a digging tool.

At that time entrance floors were just compacted sand and, as my mother and father watched, she unearthed two eggs with illegible writing on them within minutes. "See," she said, "someone has put a spell on the household. These must have been here for many years." Then she picked them up, wrapped them in a cloth, mumbled some words and burnt them.

Though my father came from Bengal, the land traditionally known in the subcontinent as "the land of magic," he was not impressed. He didn't care about who put the spell on the house or their reasons. All he wanted to do was to move out.

His new house was adjacent to the large mansion where the British ambassador lived. At one time, it had housed the famed Lawrence of Arabia and, as a child, I remember going to children's parties on the roof organized by the Legation staff. Most buildings at the time had open terraces on the top floors with "see-through" holes in their walls. These terraces or *Kharjah* served as sitting areas for the women who, traditionally, were forbidden to go out of the houses on their own. The terraces were also used as sleeping areas in the hot summer months.

My father had moved into prime real estate. A few diplomatic missions located there were our neighbors and next door was a Saudi businessman of Indian origin. His house, much larger than ours by a three to one ratio, almost touched ours on one side. A window in its wall was dead opposite one of ours, so the women of the houses sat and chatted across the three-foot gap while their sons and I played downstairs in the open ground in front of the houses. Two buildings away was an ancient mosque with a leaning minaret that had been featured in Richard Francis Burton's book, *Personal Narrative of a Pilgrimage to Al Madinah and Makkah* [sic], when he visited Arabia to perform Haj in 1853.[ii]

I was born in this new location and thus grew up without the so-called "curse." In fact, I thrived. I remember being in my pram on my usual evening outing outside the city gates when a red car went by. I recognized it as being a car from the office where my father worked. A European woman was at the wheel and her three passengers wore the usual black covering of Arab women with only their faces exposed. One sat in front beside the driver and I recognized her. She was my aunt.

I somehow knew that my mother and the housemaid were the other passengers so I called out, "Mama, *Khala, Mabruka*." (Mother, aunt and the maid servant). I kept calling until the boy handling my pram got tired of my cries and decided to take me home.

Apparently he had also recognized them so he took his sweet time to take me home and thus give them time to have their drive and be back before us.

The British consul's wife was quite friendly with my mother so this drive with my aunt into the desert beyond the city gates wasn't extraordinary. Then, in those days the authorities were quite relaxed about allowing women to drive. There were only a handful of cars so who would object to a foreign woman driving?

On this occasion when we got home, my mother and aunt were entertaining their guest and I found them laughing and chatting. To me, all that mattered was that my mother was there. She was home. I was safe. With everything normal, I went to my rocking horse and showed off my expertise.

But my mother and aunt's expeditions really were extraordinary. At that time in the Arabian Peninsula, women were expected to know their place and that place was "home." It had been that way for generations, going back to the time when they lived in tents. That was the reason for the incredible rooftop gardens and terraces—the women weren't supposed to leave the house.

I was a little boy but even then I knew the rules for me were different. My father spoiled me and I always took liberties with him. One morning when he left the house for the office in his white suit I wanted to surprise him. When he stepped onto the sandy lane just outside the house, I was in my usual good-bye place, a window with strips of wood to stop me from falling out. He looked up and waved, as he always did, but I unbuttoned my trousers and sent a stream of urine towards him.

Luckily he saw it in time and took a few steps back. He gestured, said a few threatening words and continued on to work. I was in no doubt as to what would happen to me. When he returned, I was not to be found. I hid myself in a walk-in closet but, of course, my father found me. "You are a naughty, naughty boy," he told me. "It was not a good thing you did. If you do it again, I will spank you and..."

I got off easy that time but his warning put the fear of God into me. He was that angry.

The closet also featured in another unforgettable incident. Like most people, we slept on mattresses on the floor. One night my father sat in an adjoining room but I was snuggled between my mother and my aunt. They chatted while waiting for me to go to sleep until two men stepped out of the closet only a few feet from us. One said, "Careful not to step on the child." Then they walked towards the room where my father was and promptly vanished.

My mother and aunt sat in petrified silence for a few seconds and then called hysterically to my father. He quickly made a thorough search of the house but found nothing. The house was well secured. No one could have got in or, more importantly, got out. Tired and exhausted, he crept under the mosquito netting and told them, "You must be tired. You need sleep."

What happened? My mother and aunt both swore they saw the men before they vanished into thin air. My grandmother though had an explanation. The men were *sullah al bait* or spirits that resided in old homes and protected them, maybe what we would call good spirits today.

By the standards of those times, the Kabir family was more than comfortable with everything that a family needed—even the contraption called a radio. Radios were forbidden in Saudi Arabia and thought to be instruments of the devil. The religious authorities asked how a wooden box could otherwise speak. Music was also banned and gramophone records were sacrilege. Such was the level of distrust that when my father presented a loudspeaker system to the Makkah authorities for their Holy Mosque much later, they accepted it although with great suspicion. Telephones likewise struggled for acceptance.

My father traveled a lot and met many influential people. It was part of his job and he always had interesting stories to tell when he came home. Once in the 1930s he led a delegation to visit King Abdul Aziz bin Saud at his Jeddah Palace to present a car to him. A large carpet had been put down in front of the entrance to the palace and my father and his retinue were directed to drive onto it. Seating befitting royalty had been put on another carpet and His Majesty greeted them with customary Arab hospitality. They sat for a while and were served with Arab coffee made of crushed green coffee beans and cardamom boiled together. It was a potent brew and could be uncomfortable, especially when having cup after cup.

It was served in small rounded cups without handles, and the server continued to pour until signalled to stop. Traditionally the guest covered the top with his palm and shook it as he extended it towards the server. Unfortunately that day, one member of the entourage didn't know the sign and continued to accept the flow of cardamom and crushed beans until he choked and collapsed. After numerous cups of water he recovered.

Meanwhile, one of the royal guards dressed in white, with two crossed belts studded with bullets over his chest, with pistols on his hips and a curved dagger tucked into his belt, walked in gently holding a bundle of straw and carefully laid it in front of the car.

My father was completely taken aback but before he could speak one of His Majesty's staff asked, "What does that thing eat?"

My father said something to him and they walked up to the car and from its trunk produced a can of gasoline. "This is benzene," my father told him using the Arabic word for petrol as it was then called while he showed them how to fill the car. The entire assembly looked on, fascinated by the way the "contraption" was fed. Afterwards, as no guest was allowed to leave without a gift, His Majesty gave my father a solid gold Rolex watch with His Majesty's name and picture on the dial.

I sometimes accompanied my father on his trips to Makkah [Mecca]. As the representative of the British Legation, the Union Jack fluttered proudly on his car. I always sat in the back, sometimes stretching out to sleep. Occasionally my father recited the customary holy words before entering the Holy City.

In those days the only asphalted road led to Makkah. It was perhaps ten feet wide. The ever shifting sand enveloped most of the way. At times, all four tires would sink half way down and it would need the effort of the passengers of a passing camel caravan to put the car back on the road.

On this particular day we had no trouble with sand. My father, up in front with the driver, recited holy words and I admired the dark rocky hills on either side of us that were, I would later find out, the same age as the Appalachian range in eastern North America. Herds of various animals grazed on whatever green vegetation they could find—camels, sheep, goats and mules and their young. I remember thinking, "These are new. God must have sent them down last night."

The concept of procreation was unknown. Mentally I was a virgin and at nine years old I hadn't the slightest idea about how people or animals were made.

Another time the whole family traveled to Medina in a convertible car that my father had recently acquired.

The top cover was manually operated so driving across open desert was a risky adventure. Mechanical failure could be life threatening as temperatures reached higher than one hundred twenty degrees. There was no road *per se* to Medina. The driver simply manoeuvred the dunes and followed traditional paths while his passengers trusted him. Several times we had to stop because the car had sunk into the sand or the engine had overheated. The latter wasn't a problem, but the sand problem could only be resolved by waiting for a passing camel caravan.

At intervals along the way "tea shops" made of wooden poles and thatched roofing had primitive toilet facilities (a hole in the ground) and a large earthenwar container for water.

At dusk we stopped in one of the tea shops and ate fried fish delivered daily by fishermen as the road followed the Red Sea shoreline. Sometimes the trip took several days. Most pilgrims traveled on camel caravans. Their seats on a camel's back ranged from relatively comfortable to downright luxurious. Cars or trucks were rare and owned mostly by the royals, the rich, or government.

In the late 1940s we traveled again to Medina, this time in a military truck that housed the entire family and some servants. That journey took three days. Tents were put up at night and carpets spread out while a meal was cooked. Before going to bed, my father and some of our entourage stood out under the canopy of countless stars to smoke their cigarettes. Suddenly I interrupted, "Did you see that? A falling star."

They looked up but were too late. To my luck, two more streaked across the sky. While lighting his cigarette, the driver gave me his explanation as to what they were. He said, and I believed him at the time, "Those stars were thrown by God at the devil or his associates who eavesdropped while God talked to his angels. All those stars are meant for that purpose. No devil can come close to God or his angels."

I stood and admired the dark roof above me dotted with God's infinite firepower before I crept away humbly and entered the tent. My mother was already in bed. I chose a place close to her and coiled myself behind her.[iii]

We camped near another tea shop the second night. While trying to sleep in the pin-drop silence of the desert, I heard music. Mostly it was drum beats coming from the ground. I put my ear to the ground to make sure the music came from it. It was such an eerie feeling that I got up and asked a servant what it was. He gave me his version, and I believed that too.

"That music belongs to the martyrs who died in holy battle and were buried somewhere here. They are celebrating their victory over non-believers."

I wanted to tell him that battle was more than 1400 years ago but my father interrupted. "Go back to the tent and sleep. We have to get up before dawn." It was an order so I shut my mouth and obeyed.

My question was only answered thirty or so years later when I returned to Saudi Arabia in the 1970s after the Bangladesh revolution. By now the trip to Medina was easier with asphalted dual carriage roads with exits to gas stations and restaurants. It was like being on any modern highway anywhere and the trip took less than four hours.

As we drove along this modern highway, I spotted a black Bedouin tent with a couple of camels and goats and stopped to get some fresh air. It was just before sunset and about a hundred meters away a few men danced in a circle while others beat drums. It was the same type of musical beat I'd heard decades before coming through the desert floor and had nothing to do with martyrs. On weekends, it seemed, Bedouin families drove out into the desert and partied from sunset to dawn.

My life changed again one day in 1943 when my father returned from the office full of joy and smiles.

My mother looked confused when she asked, "Did you find a treasure?"

He hugged her and in his broken Arabic broke the news, "Aeysho,[iv] we are moving to a big house, a very big house."

Then he told us that his immediate boss, Mr. Lal Shah Bokhari, was transferred back to India and my father was promoted to his position.

As a child I hardly understood the professional details but, for sure, I was overjoyed by the thought of moving to a big house like our neighbor's. But the new one turned out to be far superior in both looks and comforts. It was three times the size of our previous house and more western in design. It was much more like several others used by other legations or consulates.

Right in front of us was the diplomatic office and residence of the senior staff of the Netherlands. To our left was the British Legation and to the right was the three-storey home of the elite Saudi family, the Ali Rezas.

We moved within a week. The ground floor had a large black and white tiled hallway with several rooms for offices for my father and his staff which included an Indian doctor and his clinic. Above were three large floors, the doctor lived on the first floor, the upper two had several rooms for our living quarters. The terrace was open with two rooms for the servants. Balconies ran around three sides on all three floors. My mother took charge of laying out the living space. The second floor had a large drawing floor with exquisite furniture. The dining room table sat fourteen and there was an inbuilt wooden cupboard filled with a variety of glassware. A water carrier had come to my previous home with two four gallon cans balanced on a long stick over his shoulders. Water was only for drinking and the toilets. But our new house had tiled bathrooms with running water, commodes and wash basins. To me, it was like stepping into a new world – the water came with the same style of water carriers but was decanted into large tanks on the roof.

It took weeks to settle down and enjoy the "goodies" of our new house. I really enjoyed the rooftop terrace. At the center was the raised area with the skylight windows for the hallway below and I soon built a little "shack" for myself. I found some boards, a few flat sticks and nails and busied myself for several days. I placed all my toys into it and used my father's Players cigarette boxes for my stamp collection.

Among the various magazines that came regularly was one for me called *Heyday*. It came with a gift of a little medal that I pinned onto my shirt and wore day in and day out to show it off to my school friends. The magazine had children's stories and drawings of fairy tale characters and my father read some to me translating them into Arabic. Soon, with my father's help, I was able to struggle with a few English words and enjoy sketching some of the characters.

I was fascinated with *Heyday*'s cartoons and I made a folder of a few pages, sketching figures and copying English words with no clue to their meaning. However, I was the proud publisher of a "magazine" and I suppose that is where my literary career began.

One morning some office people arrived at the house with bundles of cloth that were so heavy that they needed two people to carry them across their shoulders. They spread them lengthwise on the second floor verandahs and when they unfolded them I saw the flags of Britain, France, the United States and Russia—the victors of World War II. They strung them together and tied them to the balcony railings allowing them to fall freely. I didn't know who or what they represented at the time but they looked magnificent on the face and sides of our house.

Our home language was Arabic. My father did not teach me Urdu or Bengali. He didn't even enlarge on my scant knowledge of English. He thought his posting to Saudi Arabia was a permanent one and that he would retire and settle there. But, in 1947, with the partition of India and the creation of Pakistan, he had to choose which nationality he'd adopt. He chose to take Pakistani citizenship and with that the Government of Pakistan asked him to establish the Pakistan embassy and assist with the settlement of a newly appointed Indian diplomat.

He came home a few weeks later with a large cloth sack. I sat beside him as he struggled to remove the metal seal and binding wire that bound the upper part of the bag. Inside were different sizes of envelopes with red seals and two large flags. I grabbed both flags and spread them out. After looking at one, I said, "This is the Egyptian flag." It was green with a crescent and a star. I didn't notice the white part on its left. It really did resemble the Egyptian flag at that time.

My father corrected me immediately. "This is the flag of a new nation called Pakistan. The other is for India."

It meant nothing to me. I hadn't the foggiest idea of what they represented and I picked up both of them and ran to the rear verandah. As I called out to our neighbor's son, I unfurled them like a small boy showing off a new toy. On August 14, 1947, my father and I went to the terrace and flew the Pakistani flag for the first time (officially) on the soil of Saudi Arabia and on the residence of the Pakistani *chargé d'affaire.* A ceremony followed and thus we commemorated the birth of a nation.

My father gave a speech to foreign diplomats, senior Indian and Saudi government officials. I will never forget that day. There were so many people assembled in our living room. They applauded what my father said, but I was too interested in the long table in the next room full of eats to listen. Suddenly the door opened between the rooms and people flooded in devouring all that they could. In the commotion I made the best of it, I didn't bother with a plate, I just grabbed and ate.

That was the official first day of Pakistan. The Indian subcontinent had now been partitioned into two separate countries. Within a year my father was called to Pakistan and reassigned—much to his surprise. I don't think my father ever thought of that possibility but government servants have no say in their tenures and move from place to place like gypsies. So I cannot say that the move back to Pakistan was a happy choice for my father.

It was, however, my mother's happiest day and overall our family was a happy one. (The photo bellows shows me with my parents and younger brother Behram.)

While my life as a child in Jeddah was idyllic in so many ways, there were occasional problems. When my parents argued, it was usually about education. On many occasions my mother insisted that we should leave Saudi Arabia and asked my father, "Do you want your son to spend his life attending to pilgrims, reading religious rituals to them and living on their handouts? That is not acceptable to me."

But my father had his own agenda for my schooling. One night, when I was about six or seven, he told me a story that sounded like a fairy tale. He and I would travel in a plane over the sea to a country called the Sudan where he had selected a beautiful school for me.

I interrupted him. "Why should I go to school there?"

"You will learn more. The schools are better where we are going."

"But I like it here. All schools are the same."

We argued some more. When he saw it becoming futile, he finally said, "Okay. Let's go and you can see for yourself. If you don't like it, we'll come back."

"What about Mama? Will she come with us?"

She agreed with my father. "That school is good. Here, you will learn nothing. There you will be a smart boy like the Europeans."

I didn't know what that meant. Europe was someplace beyond the Jeddah sand dunes but becoming European made it seem like I would become extraordinary.

When the day of our departure arrived, we drove to an open field a couple of miles from Jeddah. There were no buildings. An airplane with a propeller on each wing stood on the open desert. A few people milled around, some pouring fuel into a part of one wing while others went in and out of the aircraft or walked around it.

The only other time I had seen a plane was months before and then it had been a biplane – the type with one wing above the other, as it circled the city at about two hundred feet. The side towards me had no door and I'd seen someone sitting and waving a black stick.

Looking back, I wonder if it was some kind of military surveillance plane.

After we climbed into the plane, we settled ourselves on wooden planks that stretched from the rear of it to the front and rested our backs against the windows. The engines came to life, roaring with occasional thunderous bursts until the propellers hummed in unison and grew louder rising to a high pitch until, with a sudden thrust of power, it rolled faster and faster, rattling and shaking us mercilessly as the undercarriage negotiated the rough terrain of a makeshift runway. Then the ground receded. I looked at my father and shouted, "Look, we are flying."

We climbed higher and higher. Below, the Red Sea was blue with a few toy-like ships, journeying in different directions. The view was breathtaking. I swivelled from side to side until my neck began to hurt and I rested against my father's shoulder and slept. When I woke up hours later the sea was still there, but the engines' continuous steady humming had begun to change. Looking down I saw a coastline.

"We've arrived," my father told me.

The wheels met the ground with a bump, then the plane shook and rattled until we slowed to a halt. The engines breathed their last and all was quiet. People rushed to open the door and we walked down. One person met my father. They shook hands and embraced before he took us to a waiting car and we drove to the railway station. We had landed at Port Sudan and would take the train journey to Khartoum.[v]

Before we arrived my father shed his western clothes and put on typical Indian khaki cloth pajamas and a shirt. Before slipping into his pyjamas, he found a little tear on the rear. Nevertheless he put them on and bending forward asked me to check if anything showed. I told him the shirt would cover the tear and thus he was transformed to a poor Indian travelling with his son. Some locals met us at Khartoum and we spent that night with one of them and then drove to Umdurman, not far from Khartoum. There we were the guests of a large man dressed in white flowing robes on top of which he was enveloped in a loose bed sheet like garment. On his head he wore a large white turban, Sudanese style. He was gracious and friendly and his baritone voice could be heard several feet away. After a feast of a lunch, he and my father walked about in the courtyard that housed several goats, chicken and some cattle.

I was tired and had no one to talk to. I must have slept for a couple of hours when my father woke me up to have tea. A few hours after sunset we had another lavish meal — barbequed goat with rice. There was no electricity, only hurricane lamps everywhere. An hour or so after our meal, they were extinguished and pin-drop silence followed.

We slept in the open on straw-made high chairs the full length of a person. Mosquitoes troubled me. I covered myself from head to toe allowing a narrow slit exposing my eyes. Above was the universe in all its splendour and glory. Stars, big and small. Some twinkled, others didn't and I remember wondering why they were different.

The next morning after breakfast our giant-like host picked me up and put me on a stool. From a plate he picked up a few grains of wheat and dropped one by one onto my head. Then he whispered, like he was saying something to himself, before putting those grains in my mouth and asking me to chew and eat them. I obeyed as he watched.

I stood still not knowing what that ceremony was about. My father looked on sipping tea. The man then asked me to open my mouth wide. I first thought that he wanted to check if I had eaten the grains. I obeyed. He felt my teeth and, at the front top centre where I have a gap, inserted his finger and held one of my front teeth firmly and shook it hard, again whispering something. As he put me down from the stool, he said in Arabic, "God bless you. Go, no one will ever harm you."

I did not understand the significance of that ritual until later, as we drove to the school, my father said, "You are lucky to be blessed by his holiness. What he did was to confer upon you a prayer to protect you from all harm and ill-wishers. There will be a guardian to look after you. Anyone who tries to harm you will receive a severe punishment."[vi]

We reached the school. Young boys, with minimal clothing on them, seemed everywhere and my father left. The next day he came back to check if I was comfortable. I cried and asked him to take me away.

"Why?' he asked.

"They take their baths in the sand," I said with tears running down my face.

My father laughed and after looking at the boys wrestling and playing in a sand pit decided that the place was not for me. He knew that I would not be able to adjust. I was glad and when we returned to Khartoum he admitted me to Comboni, the missionary school that boasts of having educated many great leaders.

The magnificent school buildings sprawled hundreds of feet in all directions. The dormitory was long and spacious with rows of beds spaced several feet apart covered with fresh white linen. The dining room was long with rectangular tables seating eight, covered with crisp table cloths, white china and shining cutlery. I had never seen or experienced anything like this before. Back in Saudi Arabia we had a dining table but ate with our hands. Only when we had guests was the cutlery displayed.

It was all too new to me, a boy from the desert. I was in heaven, or so I thought.

Nearly all the boarders were Christian. I was one of only three Muslims, and the fun part happened when the Christian students went to Church every morning before breakfast. We three raced to the tuck shop to enjoy a kind of bun laced with sugar and sesame. A glass of milk accompanied this treat. One boy a few years older than me was friendly and always paid for these morning delights. Much later, when someone by that faintly remembered name became the Prime Minister of the Sudan, I knew it had to be that boy in the school tuck shop who shared buns and glasses of milk. I have not had the opportunity to meet him since.

A year or so later, while I played football, someone came from the office and told me to report to the visitors' room. "Your father is here," he said. I followed him, more than glad, because I hadn't seen my father in several months.

He hugged me, "Are you alright? Are you happy?"

"Very happy. The school is good." I replied in English, the language of the school.

My father seemed too full of news to notice. "I have come to take you back to Jeddah, your mother is missing you."

I switched to Arabic. "But I like it here. Can I come back after a few days?"

"I don't think so, but," he paused, "we will see once we get back."

He had already spoken to the Principal and he told me he would return the next day to pick me up. "Pack all your things and any school books you were given."

I spent the rest of the day in a gloomy state. I didn't have an appetite for dinner. All I could think about was the happiness I'd experienced at Comboni – something the young and impressionable me had not experienced before.

As an adult, thinking back to that time, feeling the loss of the school and being deprived of it, I have many questions but I was simply a pawn in my father's diplomatic activities. He must have achieved his objective there and my schooling at Comboni was no longer relevant. Even after all these years, I feel it was not a fair thing to do.

He had cut the umbilical cord of my learning. As far as he was concerned his *mission* was complete. But what about the mission that he and mother set into motion? I remember my mother's words to this day. She wanted me "*to be like the Europeans, an enlightened boy.*"

I often wondered why I had to go to the Sudan in the first place. Several years after my father passed away, when I went through his diaries and collection of notes and scribbles, I came across some references about his Sudan visits. "Sudan. I went there with him," I remembered. It hit an emotional cord. I sifted through the papers.

In these he wrote: "Sending Hasan to school there [Comboni] was a perfect reason for my many trips. I was only visiting my son." In another entry he referred to meeting a friend who hosted him "and provided him with what he had come for." What exactly was that? He mentioned "the treasure of words he carried to his

Sahib." These so pleased the Sahib that he was sent back for more and then "the Sahib's Sahib promoted me to a higher rank and showered me with gifts." The word Sahib always meant a superior person or boss. In my father's case, it obviously meant someone higher up in the British diplomatic service. But what kind of a mission?

It was 1944 and early 1945 and WII was on. *Were his trips some kind* of *intelligence work for the British?* It is only very recently that I've discovered that my father may have ferreted out the Nazi's supply lines for their troops in the desert. In one of papers he writes, *"I was responsible for the discovery in 1943, of the route through which all the vital necessities of life, supplied to the Sudanese by the Anglo-American powers during the war, were being smuggled out of the Sudan to the enemy occupied countries – Ethiopia and Eritrea."* He further added that he had *"helped the authorities concerned in discovering the route through which slave traffic between Baluchistan and Saudi Arabia was carried out."*

At that time I thought that my father knew that my education would be better in Jeddah though in his heart he knew that no schooling worth its name existed in Saudi Arabia. Instead of learning, I spent the day cycling on dirt roads with my neighbors' sons and sitting, totally bored, in class. [vii]

Obviously I was too young to think philosophically but, perhaps, my gloom that evening in the Sudan expressed the concealed yearning which exists in every human. For most people, the chance to climb the ladder of life is very rare. Only those few who pursue it with their determination to break away from a medieval-like routine life, who rough it out, will emerge shining with successes. Time and circumstances did not allow me to take that road.

After the partition of the subcontinent, my father was posted back to Karachi, Pakistan in 1949.

I remember disembarking from the ship and, while my father, mother, brother and sister trailed behind, racing to a black car that was larger than anything I had seen in Jeddah. The driver opened the rear door and I made sure I occupied the window seat. My father handed over the list of our luggage to one of the men and I waited impatiently until we drove to Khawaja Shahabuddin's residence. He was the Minister of Education at the time and the younger brother of the Governor General of Pakistan. His daughter had married my uncle, my father's younger brother. [viii] We spent a couple of hours there and then drove to the temporary accommodation that our host had arranged for us – the Baluch Mess, a military guest house. Days later we moved into an apartment on Preedy Street and my father immediately put me into boarding school.

There were many old well established schools in Karachi, most of them affiliated with universities in the United Kingdom, but he chose a smaller school run by Mr. Colaco and his wife. The Marie Colaco School in Saddar took students from kindergarten to grade 7. The boarders totalled six including their two children, Claude and Noel. When I first entered the school with my father, classes were on. The courtyard was empty. We were ushered into an office and sat in front of a large desk with stacks of paper piled up on one side while we waited for someone to come.

On the wall was a picture of a man in Arab-like clothing with flowing hair and a beard. He had a handsome, kind-looking face. As I had come from a land of flowing white robes, I immediately thought that was he must be the principal of the school. I kept staring at the picture. There was something odd about it. I could not understand why he had a drawing of a heart across his chest colored in red. It was quite strange.

The door suddenly opened and a very smart good looking woman entered. She was dressed in a blouse and skirt like most Arab women. My mother also dressed in that fashion, so it was nothing new and helped settle me. My father got up to meet her and we all shook hands. She introduced herself as Miss Thadani, the principal. I felt disappointed. I had expected the man with the flowing hair and beard and I wondered who the Arab-looking man was.

In the following days I discovered it was a picture of Jesus Christ and I remember thinking to myself, "So that is what he looked like." Coming out of Saudi

Arabia as a raw eleven year old unfamiliar with drawings or any form of representation of holy images or statues of religious figures, this was something totally new to me. I had been taught all about Jesus and Moses etc. in Saudi Arabia but the law did not permit pictures of them.

My father had previously visited the school and explained my Arabic education and my deficiency in the English language. After a brief conversation with him, Miss Thadini looked at me and smiled, "Come with me."

I took her hand and we marched out of her office and straight into an ongoing classroom. As we entered the whole class stood and said with one voice, "Good morning Miss." The classroom teacher walked up to her and after exchanging a few words, Miss Thadini left.

I looked around. There were boys and girls aged six or seven. The class room teacher, a young woman took me by the hand and sat me in the front row. Around me were pupils half my size and age.

For a boy out of the desert, having previously attended schools with only male students and teachers dressed in white robes, this was completely different and fascinating. It was a new environment where men, women, boys and girls were all together.

My knowledge of English was almost zero. When the class teacher stood beside me and asked my name, I looked back at her and confidently mimicked, "What is your name?" It was like an echo of her question.

The class murmured and giggled but the teacher turned around and, with a finger to her lips, gave a warning look. After this assessment of my deficiency in English she took special attention to guide me into a language completely foreign to me from then on.

English was not really too foreign, as I already had been introduced briefly to it in the Comboni School in Khartoum and through *Heyday*. But sadly, my return to Jeddah and its Arabic medium of education had adversely affected the little I had learned. However recollections of certain words and sentences came back to me, and within months I was able to converse and write as a kindergarten student would. Being a boarder, I had the advantage of learning faster as English was the only language spoken day and night. Within a year, I was promoted to grade three. I excelled in mathematics and in one test, the teacher gave me 102 out of 100. It couldn't be a mistake, could it? I must have been *good*.

The boarding facilities were a makeshift arrangement. Not a true dormitory – just an empty room. We had to carry our mattresses from a store room in the courtyard and spread them on the allocated space provided. On one corner was an iron spring bed on which a senior male teacher who shared our room slept.

In all we were six boarders. Three brothers, Anwar, Munawar and Sarwar, apparently were the relatives of the ruler of the Princely State of Bahawalpur plus the two children of Mr. and Mrs Colaco and me.[ix] While lying on the floor, my thoughts went back to my brief experience in Khartoum when I was six or seven.

Saudi boys wore flowing robes and looked bored with life. Coming to school for them had been a necessity. They sat through religious-oriented classes. Only a few minutes of some periods were spent teaching mathematics and geography. Nothing else. Those subjects were perhaps a luxury for religious teachings were the primary curriculum. It was the order of the day then and, unbelievably, still exists. It seems so sad that after decades of the advancement of sciences worldwide that about 60% of schooling in the 21st century is religiously oriented.

I feel sorry for great minds that are doomed to remain in mental stagnation.

But that was not my worry at the time. Being in the Marie Colaco School was a leap forward as far as my education was concerned. I had been uncomfortable with the set up but I had roughed it out as I was determined to succeed. It was like an adventure and I was ready to accept any hardship if I was to accomplish my goal to have a place in this new world. I had to fight to survive.

Gradually I began merging my "Sudan days" with my new educational situation. Here a whiff of that, there a bit of this and, as time moved on I was very much at home despite certain inconveniences. I made many friends. And, because of one who took piano lessons, I found the world of music. I will never forget my Russian teacher. Her ruler hit my knuckles every time I made a mistake and I would play on with a nonchalant expression and continue to enjoy the sound of the piano.

I actually came to enjoy every minute at the school. I had friends and I played football and cricket and participated in athletics. But suddenly one morning, my father came to the school and I was summoned to the principal's office. It was déjà vu. As in the Sudan, he asked me to pack up my belongings without giving any reason.

I was not happy. The school had become my home and I now knew I wanted a steady and continuous schooling. But we were going to Mumbai. Another change, another new home and, worse, another new school.

ENDNOTES

[i] Later, with British help, the Sharif's family established the Hashemite Kingdoms of Jordan and Iraq.

[ii] I saw the iconic mosque when I returned to Jeddah in the early 1970s but authorities demolished it some

years later. Unofficially I was told that authorities didn't like the way it looked — old and dilapidated. I could have told them that they didn't realize what they had lost.

[iii] In 2010, when I began writing this book, I retraced that trip and while we were stopped at a teashop I was talking to a banker friend when we witnessed a few showers of falling stars. To my surprised he told me the same thing I had heard more than sixty years earlier.

[iv] My mother's first name was Ayesha but my father always called here Aeysho when he was in a happy mood. Otherwise it was "Sitti," the Arabic word for respected one or madam.

[v] Many years later when I moved to Saudi Arabia in the 70s, on one of the street of Jeddah a Dakota DC3 or DC2 I am not sure stood perched on a high concrete column as an exhibit, a museum piece just like the aircraft I travelled on to Port Sudan with my father. Perhaps it was the very one!

[vi] Later I came to know that 'the big man' was the great grandson of the *Mehdi,* a religious leader of the time when General Gordon of the Sudan was assassinated.

[vii] Paved roads did not exist at that time. The only asphalted road was between Jeddah and Makkah and

that was barely ten feet wide mostly covered by shifting sand.

[viii] A police officer at the time, he (my uncle) later rose to the rank of Inspector General of Police.

[ix] Bahawalpur was one of the several Princely States Pakistan inherited after the partition of the subcontinent. India, too, inherited several Princely States. Several years later, both in India and Pakistan they were merged within the political framework and their Princely status.

2

Our new home in Mumbai was not exactly a home.

We lived in the Sea Face Hotel on Marine Drive in two bedrooms, a sitting room and one toilet. Only a dual carriage road and a wide pedestrian area separated us from the sea. Several miles across on the other side of the bay was a long formation known as Malabar Hill where the rich and elite lived, including the founder of Pakistan, Mr. Muhammad Ali Jinnah. The Towers of Silence, the Parsi burial ground, was also on that hill. The view from our hotel balcony was picturesque—multi-storey buildings lined the Drive and just across the road to our left was the famed Brabourne Cricket Stadium.

My father wasted no time in admitting us to boarding schools. My brothers, Behram and Reda, and I went to St. Mary's High School and my sisters to the Sacred Heart Convent School.

St. Mary's was a Jesuit operated school

with a large cathedral-like church at one end and its buildings – the dormitory, dining hall and classrooms and the playgrounds were, as we said in those days, "out of this world" and even more impressive than the Comboni School in the Sudan. I was admitted into class IV, a tribute to the teaching I had received at the Marie Colaco School. Initially I felt a bit below the academic standard but after a few months I felt comfortable. A year later, in 1951, I got a double promotion to class VI and to my surprise, on Prize Day, I received a book, *Uncle Tom's Cabin* for drawing.

Our study hall was on the first floor of the main building and on the weekend when we stayed in school, I spent hours reading books from the library and writing letters to my family. I also indulged myself trying to write a personal journal. It is so amusing to read those pages now. Once, with typical juvenile pomposity I began, "The rain was raining..." (Please don't laugh. It was perhaps one of my first expressions of a latent desire to be a writer.)

Books opened my world. The first I took from the library was *Robinson Crusoe* by Daniel Defoe and it made me try to find other books of adventure and mystery. I added comics such as *Superman, Captain Marvel* and the like and they gradually hooked me and led to the more serious writing of H.G. Wells, Jules Verne, Arthur C. Clark as well and thus I plunged into the debatable subject of UFOs.

At this school, students were divided into four groups called houses. I was in the Ogilvies. Boarders received a quarterly merit card evaluating their performances in sports, academics and behavior. A white card was the best; pink was the worst. I received white cards throughout my stay and one year was selected to be the Ogilvies prefect. That meant I led the house in a military-like formation to various destinations, such as study hall, the dining room, and the dormitories. It was a great honor and I was proud of myself.

The school allowed us to spend weekends with our parents. I took a bus to stop in front of the Eros Cinema opposite the Church Gate Railway Station that was close to where my parents lived. After catching up on family business, I read my favorite adventure strips like Mandrake the Magician from the newspaper supplements.

I still remember the voice of a poor boy almost my own age who sang every Sunday below our hotel. I watched him play the harmonium and sing "Oh Sunday, Oh Sunday" with passers-by handing him some alms. He would look up and wave a hand. I did not have much to give but I decided to spare some coins, so I wrapped them in a piece of paper and dropped the package down from our balcony. He looked up and gave a gesture of thanks. This became a weekly routine and I looked forward to his appearance. Sometimes I waited for him before he even arrived.

After lunch my routine was to head for the matinee at the Odeon cinema. Opposite was a kiosk with the latest comic books near the Taj hotel and I must have bought hundreds of them – *Captain Marvel, Tom Mix, Hopalong Cassidy, Gene Autry* and *The lone Ranger* and the like. I was more than happy. School was great. While I took a keen interest in sports like football and various field events in general, I excelled in the one hundred yard sprint and obstacle races and always stood above the numeral 1 on the victory stand.

Then one morning someone came to me and told me that I had a guest in the parlor. Who could that be? I couldn't imagine, but when I saw my father at that odd time on a normal working day, I knew what he was there to do. *I had seen it before*. His arrivals at odd hours meant only one thing. "Pack up."

He had a guilty look on his face as he handed me a package of sweets. Perhaps it was a bribe. Perhaps it was his way of paving the way into having the courage of saying the words I so dreaded to hear. "Hasan," he said. "I am sorry but you have to leave school. We are going back to Karachi and from there to Iraq."

Karachi? I'd been there before at the Marie Colaco School and I'd left good friends behind. But Iraq? I didn't even know where it was. I was firmly anchored at St. Mary's, and this meant another disastrous beak-away.

Reflecting back, it seems most unfortunate that the diplomatic service did no justice to the educational continuity of its diplomats' children. I felt especially despondent. I had started at zero on the educational scale at a late age and struggled so hard to catch up for those lost years in Jeddah. Once again I was in the same situation as when I returned to Saudi Arabic from the Sudan before I went to Marie Colaco and St. Mary's.

For the first few months in Iraq I sat at home. There were no western type schools and I was later admitted to an all-Arabic language school. Though I spoke the language, my vocabulary was not at the same level as that in my class and mentally I was tuned to a different educational frequency. I was most unhappy.

My mother stepped in and forced my father to get me out of that mess and find me a western education. For the next couple of months, letters flew back and forth between Iraq, the United Kingdom and Pakistan. I was accepted by one school in England and two in Pakistan. My father felt that as I had never had the Pakistani or "home" experience, he should put me into a Pakistani school, but the schools that accepted me were not ones that he had in mind. He wanted something better for me and one of his friends suggested the Burn Hall School.

Burn Hall, founded by the Mill Hill Brothers from Ireland, had many decades of educational presence in the subcontinent of India.

It had been established in Baramulla, Kashmir in 1901, before relocating to Abbottabad in the North West Frontier province of Pakistan. It was 4300 feet above sea level and had picturesque mountain views. At that time it had one hundred boarders and another hundred boy and girls between the ages of six and eleven were day students.

There was bad news at first. Burn Hall didn't want me. Its admission period has passed and it was suggested that my father try again the following year. The school catered for the children of the elite and the sons of senior military personnel. It never had problems filling its few vacancies. My father, however, was not without influence. His brother had married the daughter of the Governor of the province, Khawaja Shahabuddin who had been the Minister of Education when we had arrived from Jeddah. He was very helpful and I was admitted without further fuss.

The Fathers who set up the school realized that if the

new nation of Pakistan was to do well, it would need men of high caliber. These they defined as intelligent, strong-willed, determined, nationalistic and with the highest level of integrity. The English public school system had built the British Empire, so the Fathers replicated that system. They believed that sports built character and therefore promoted games such as cricket, hockey (on grass), football, tennis and athletics. Burn Hall went on to produce top civil servants, diplomats, professors, teachers, generals and businessmen. How proud I am to be part of it. I thank my parents, especially my mother, for my education there.

To my surprise, my determination to learn and the bits and pieces of schooling since my days at Marie Colaco and St. Mary's qualified me for admittance to class VII at Burn but, oh my word, I had to work hard. When I'd entered Marie Colaco I was basically illiterate and had started in Kindergarten although I was eleven. It had been very embarrassing. Now, at Burn Hall, I was undaunted and I resolved to face any challenges as courageously as possible. My parents had finally put me into a school with the right motto: *Quo Non Ascendum*, meaning To What Heights Can I Not Rise!

By the time I turned sixteen in 1954 I had caught up the lost years and now had to face the University of Cambridge Overseas School Certificate examination. Before the results came I found out that I'd been admitted to the prestigious Government College in

Lahore together with some of my classmates, though most of my class had chosen the armed services. I was overjoyed – until I heard that I'd failed English in the Cambridge exam. As a result I had to return to school and repeat the year.

The Burn Hall's principal, Father J. KLaver, was sympathetic. He asked the Cambridge examiners to re-evaluate my paper again but they refused. I had to accept that I'd need to repeat the entire year. I was sad, but there were compensations. The school decided to divide students into four sports teams to compete against each other year round. That year to my delight, one was named after me and in 1955, the Hasan Kabir team competed against the Ralph Cross, Imtiaz and Mahboob teams.[i]

BURN HALL SCHOOL

GAMES

AWARDED TO

Hassan Kabir (Captain)

of

Hassan Kabir's Champion Team.

1955

Sportsmaster.

I kept myself busy that year with hobbies—philately and photography. I had a dark room for developing my films and I converted my father's old folding type as an enlarger. I spent a month during the summer trekking with friends in the mountainous areas of Kaghan, camping at the legendary lake known as Saif ul Mulk and further north at Lake Lulusar, a magnificent lake sandwiched between mountains. Before I knew it, it was time to study hard for the examinations again and this time I not only passed, I achieved the Credit standard in English. I'd been lucky. One of the optional topics allowed us to write a fictional story and I'd jumped at that.

At Lake Lulusar that past summer I'd crawled into my sleeping bag with only my face open to the tapestry of the heavens above.

I will never forget that sight. Countless dots of light,

some larger than the others all, except a few, blinking. There was a river of concentrated light that ran right across the sky that I later learned was the Milky Way. My thoughts went wild as I absorbed the wonders far above me. *I wish I could go there*, I said to myself and as I tried to absorb the majesty of the infinite worlds above, my interest in the cosmos was born.

Then something disturbed my thoughts. It came from the lake and sounded as though a large wave splashed close to us. I looked, but there was nothing. The splash came again a couple of minutes later but this time I didn't bother to look. It was getting cold and I preferred to snuggle into the warmth of my sleeping bag.

So later in the examination room, my story came easily: *As I lay beside the lake, a man dressed like a warrior with some kind of lance extended towards me, rode a lion the size of a horse* etc. etc. I wrote and wrote, filling several pages. I got so involved it felt like I was narrating a true event.

But I made it through the exam. Although my command of English was far from perfect, I had finished with school and was ready for college. With my School Leaving Certificate from Cambridge I was admitted into the second year of the Faculty of Arts at the prestigious Government College in Lahore

and when it came to select my subjects, I chose Physics, Mathematics, Astronomy and Geography. Furthermore I was brave enough to do the Bachelor degree with Honors in Geography.

When I told my father what my choices were he wrote back with an emphatic NO. “Take subjects such as economics, geography, French or Arabic. These will help you compete in the Civil or Foreign Service Examination.” He wanted me to follow in his path and become a civil servant. He also sent a letter to the principal of my college.

The end of my academic freedom came when the principal called me into his office. “Your father,” he told me, “wrote and has asked me to advise you to prepare yourself for the Civil Service Competitive Examination once you do your Master’s. What will you do with Astronomy and Physics? You will only become a schoolteacher or a college lecturer with poor pay and a routine life with my no great future to look forward to." He got up from his desk and walked around and then stood in front of me. "Look, I know your family's background. All your uncles are doing extremely well as civil servants. In India, West and East Pakistan, the Kabir family has achieved respect and admiration. I am proud to say your uncle in India, Professor Humayun Kabir, was with me at Oxford University. Today he is a Cabinet Minister. So think positive. Your father wants the best for you. Therefore, I am changing your subjects and from tomorrow you start your new classes." He paused and then added, "Please come back and see me whenever you want to talk. Good luck."

I had lost command of my life. Perhaps it was customary, the traditional imposition of a path to follow that elders make without realizing the inner feelings or needs of their loved ones. They think they are doing their best. They may sincerely think so, but they frequently do not realize the hurt they cause or how they harm the latent intellectual progress of their progeny. As a result families frequently remain stagnant in one kind of activity and the chance to advance to pursue higher intellectual achievements in another field is lost.

At times and in some parts of the world, minds broke away from such traditional thinking. The Renaissance is one example when there seems to have been breakthroughs in almost every form of human endeavor known at the same time. Yet so many nations resist change and are warped by their allegiance to customs and ways of thought that suit a way of life that existed a thousand years ago. Stubborn leaders who adhere to archaic thinking have no place in the twenty-first century world. They increasingly turn to violence and thought-control to dominate their peoples. I think it's pathetic, evil and monstrous.

However, back to my university days. I went on to gain the highest marks in my B.A./ B.Sc degree and was awarded a Medal of Distinction and a government scholarship to pursue my Master's in the same field. Whatever the obstacles, I had lived up to the Burn Hall motto—*Quo non Ascendum*.

At least, up to that time.

When I think back to the day when I took the Geography Honors Practical Exams, I realize now it was the moment that changed the course of my life. I sat comfortably at the desk with my well sharpened pencils, an eraser, ruler and pen all neatly arranged in front of me. It was May 08, 1959 and I was ready for all he mathematical questions, graphs and the like that were to come.

Prior to any examination I usually compose myself so that I'm not distracted. However, that day it was different. The exam was in a long hall in the Geography Department. Students, male and female, sat at two tables with a small passage between them. I sat at the larger table and two girls sat diagonally across from me at the small table. I looked at them once or twice as they chatted in low whispers.

From the way they spoke and occasionally giggled, I deduced they were close friends. They were well dressed and their behavior fitted the conservative upbringing of well-to-do upper middle class families. Both looked attractive. One did most of the talking and the other looked like she was a good listener.

Somehow she made an impression on me. I wanted to get to know her. Something inside me kept saying, *That's the girl.*

Then a serious-looking woman marched into the hall with a pile of papers. She dropped the heavy load on the table in front of me, pushed back her glasses, then distributed the papers. I read mine twice. Of the seven questions, I knew six and we only had to answer four. It was easy! I marked the ones I knew would take the longest to answer in the three hours and set to work. An hour and a bit later I was finished.

I sat comfortably and reread my answers, unaware that I was being watched. I folded my answers but the talkative girl bravely walked over to me and asked to borrow my eraser and when the invigilator stepped out of the room, she asked, "What's the answer for question four?"

I spread my papers for her to see and I saw her scan whatever she could. She returned to her seat and told her friend what she had seen. Then the invigilator returned and I took my papers up to her. She refused to accept them until the half time point was reached. I had to wait, but it turned out to be lucky because the girls finished as well. I'd thought I might have a chance to talk with them but after a brief "Hello" they left. I wondered if I'd ever meet them again. The chances were slim. Almost nonexistent, or so I thought.

The head of the Department of Geography at Government College had been my teacher for the past three years and admired my love of his subject. He always welcomed me to "talk geography" and he had to approve all applications for graduate work at the University of the Punjab. He and I were in conversation when three girls entered his office.

Two were the same girls from my examination, including the one I was so attracted to. It was a treat because they also asked permission to apply for admission to the university for their Masters' degrees. They had to have recognized me but I could not tell that by their reaction. Even after we were all admitted and began attending classes, we never talked. During breaks between classes I used to sit in the library and write up notes on the lecture I'd just attended. Everything seemed hopeless.

A breakthrough came one afternoon when Dr. Saiduddin, the head of the University geography department, called them into his office to tell them he needed a reception committee for a delegation from the Dhaka University's geography department. He suggested they add a male and they selected me. I felt elevated and from then on the three of them and I became a team and firm friends. We were inseparable.

Let me introduce them.

The one who had borrowed my eraser in the Examination Hall was attractive and pleasant and somehow always took the lead in conversations. Her name was Sughra. The second was also very pleasant and good-looking who ended all her sentences with a bit of laughter. Her name was Najma. The third, named Rasheda, had been in the Examination Hall with Sughra.

Rasheda was the one I'd admired at first sight and I came to know that she was brilliant. She'd scored the highest mark in the Honors exams and I wondered if the bit of help I'd given Sughra had meant anything because I'd come second. However, as my overall marks were higher, I'd been first in the university and thus won the medal.

As we got to know each other more intimately something within me kept saying, *Don't lose her.*

A few months into my first year the university had a special convocation for those who achieved Awards of Distinction. Both President General Mohammad Ayub Khan and the visiting Prime Minister of Iran were the chief guests. It was a special and joyous day for me.

Then election fever started bubbling throughout the university. A senior student persuaded me to stand for the Joint Secretary position. I hadn't a clue as to what it would be involved but my female friends and some others persuaded me and the publicity machine swung into action. Seven of us stood for Joint Secretary. With the help of my friends I travelled to towns and cities outside Lahore to canvas for support. I was well and truly in the limelight. The girls, including one of their friends from the history department, guaranteed that the women would vote for me. I felt both elated and responsible at the same time. They trusted me to represent their best interests.

I won by a margin of seventy-eight votes. The friend who had suggested that I run also won and we jointly celebrated. The university cafeteria must have made more money that night than on any other occasion. Then, after that was over, our "gang of four," the three girls and I, decided to have a party of our own in my newly acquired office. It was glorious.

Even more glorious was the fact that my relationship with Rasheda built into a serious and reciprocal romance. On the 12th of April 1961, the day of Yuri Gagarin's flight into space, we confessed our love to each other. She picked up a pen and on my right wrist traced the letters I L U, joining the I with a line to the top of the L and then from the bottom of the L to the U. That became our logo. She went over the word several times with the pen.

Two days later things became more serious. Just after class, as I escorted her to her waiting car, I said, "Let's get married." She looked surprised but said nothing. A meeting with her mother was arranged a month later.

I waited nervously in her living room, wondering if she'd be friendly or hostile. Rasheda's younger sister entered with a class of fruit juice and then disappeared.

Finally Rasheda's mother came. I scrambled to my feet and waited for her to sit. She pointed to the sofa next to her. She must have been told that my grasp of the Urdu language was tenuous because our conversation was half-English, half-Urdu.

"What are your future plans? I'm told you are going to try for the Foreign Service."

"Yes."Service would keep you out of the country, I want my daughter to be near me."

I didn't know how to respond. She pointed to my glass of fruit juice and while I took a few sips she went on, "Why not look for a position with a commercial organization like Esso?[ii] That is a prestigious job and they pay well."

I shook my head in a way that showed I sort of approved and promised that I'd try just to shorten the conversation. Then we talked about my parents and life in general. The interview was neither a failure nor a success—at least that was my analysis. But Rasheda told me the next day that her mother liked me. I had scored.

However, I never gave up my Foreign Service ambition. It would be difficult. I knew that. As a student with only a B.A. to my name, I'd compete against others with masters and doctorates. However, I passed the exam with an extraordinarily high mark in the oral section and a scrape-through pass on the written section. Furthermore, that year, the civil service exams for were the Civil and Foreign Service only. Other government positions, such as police, customs, and railways, were excluded. Any other year I might have qualified for a job in one of those. It was not meant to be.

Life goes on, however, the secretary of the University Union resigned and the Vice Chancellor appointed me to replace him. I hosted two important events during my tenure. One was for H.H. Prince Karim Agha Khan who visited Lahore.

Professors, some senior officials and students attended his grand reception and, in appreciation, he donated a large sum of money for the improvement of the University Cafeteria. The second event was the visit of the Dave Brubeck Jazz Band and the evening we organized was packed with music lovers.

Summer vacation was around the corner and some suggested a trip to India, I vetoed it as I had taken that journey only three summers ago after passing my Faculty of Arts Examination. I settled for an adventure with two friends (one from Malaysia, the other from Singapore) to hitchhike across India from Lahore to Kolkata (formerly Calcutta). They had ulterior motives. Steamships home were cheaper from Kolkata than from Karachi.

After crossing the border to enter India at Amritsar we got our first ride on a truck carrying some goats, a cow and some chickens. That night we stopped at a small village where after our dinner of eggs, bread and tea, we slept on long wooden benches with tablecloths from the restaurant as sheets. I remember hoping that it wouldn't rain and, after a breakfast of lentils and bread, we set off again.

Every now and then we asked for directions and as the days passed by, we became tired. On some occasions when we were allowed onto "puller" carts drawn by oxen we took advantage of the slow progress to stretch and snatch some sleep. Finally we reached a village just fifty miles from Kolkata. We walked to the railway station and pleaded with an employee to get a free ride because we were poor university students.

He looked us over, accepted our plea and after talking to the ticket collector generously accommodated us in third class. Once we reached Howrah Station in Kolkata, he came to our compartment, led us to the exit and said something to the ticket collector. This example of courtesy and generosity was typical of everyone we met during that trip. However, that was the summer of 1957 and I wonder if such a trip would be possible in today's political climate. I certainly hope so.

My friends and I parted company at the railway station and I took a cycle rickshaw to my Uncle Jahangir Kabir's address. Crossing the Hooghly River was like crossing an ocean. The Hooghly Bridge was renamed in 1965 as Rabindra Setu after Rabindranath Tagore, the Indian Nobel Laureate. My uncle's address was also renamed. I had gone to 10A Congress Exhibition Road and that became 10A Humayun Kabir Road after my uncle, the younger brother of my father, who was a poet, a philosopher and an Indian ex-cabinet minister.

I ran out of money in Kolkata so I telegraphed a friend back in Lahore. The address read "To Ninoo, Outside Casino, The Mall Road, Lahore. Please send Rupees 200 at..." Ninoo was a close and generous friend who daily parked himself and his friends outside a popular restaurant and night club called the Casino to spend the night gossiping and feasting. As such, he was an icon. My telegram reached him and he sent the rupees promptly.

By myself now, I took a train to East Pakistan which

is now Bangladesh for my first visit to the area as an adult. I had some uncles there and thus I had an opportunity to meet them and my paternal grandmother whom I hadn't seen since I was seven. After this reunion in Dhaka I took the train further on to Chittagong to meet my youngest uncle, Feroze Kabir.

He took me to see the picturesque tribal areas and the Cox's Bazaar beach. It extends in all direction and its soft white sand melts through one's fingers. We only stayed there for two days as I was a desert boy and not too fond of the sea. Back in Chittagong we went for a meal at one of my uncle's friends, Mrs. Douple. We sat on her balcony, enjoying refreshing drinks before dinner, while our hostess's daughter played Dvorak's *Humoresque* on the piano. I hadn't heard of Dvorak to this point but my ears had already been tune to appreciate classical music by my time in my various school.

After dinner we were served Turkish coffee in little cups. When I finished mine and tried to place the cup on the table, Mrs. Douple asked for it. She shook it gently in a circular motion and placed it upside down on an angle in the saucer.

My uncle knew exactly what she was up to. "She's going to read your future."

After a few minutes she picked it up and began humming to herself.

"You must write down what she is going to tell you,"

my uncle said before calling to her daughter, "Zarina, get us some paper and pencil."

When she gave them to me, Zarina said, "Good luck. Mother is very good."

Mrs. Douple concentrated on what was in the cup as though she were in a trance. Finally she began talking and I wrote down everything she said. Sometimes she spoke so quickly, it became difficult to keep up but in the end I had written forty-five items that were mainly predictions about my person life such as:

My first house would have a slanting red roof. This came true when I moved into a house allotted to me in 1966 by the Company I worked with.

My wife's name would begin with an R. As it did.

My daughter's name would begin with an S. Again, this became true.

You will live in many land and in one of them people will wear an unusual headdress. Again this became true when I moved to Saudi Arabia.

There were many more, obviously and I still have that list I scribbled down.

Days later, I returned to Kolkata via Dkaha after another visit to my grandmother. When I said my good-byes, she placed her hand on my head and said something in Bengali that I didn't understand. Then she handed me a gold ring with a ruby stone surrounded my three little *Ferozas*, (Turquoise) green stones, on each side. One of my aunts translated her message. My grandmother wanted me to have it because it had been given to her by her mother when she got married. The ring was a family heirloom and my grandmother had a special affection for me because my mother was an Arab from the Holy Land.

I returned to Kolkata to the home of my uncle Jahangir Kabir. He was a politician and a businessman with a large farm with fruit trees out of the city. After my first daughter was born he named the fruit tree grove after her – Shahnaz Bagh or Shahnaz Garden. Uncle Jahangir's children reached great heights in commercial organizations and law. One of his daughters became a judge in the Kolkata High Court and a son rose to serve as the Chief Justice of the Indian Supreme Court.

Another uncle, Humayun Kabir happened to be visiting Kolkata at the time and offered to take me along with him to New Delhi. As he was in Prime Minister Jawaharlal Nehru's cabinet as Minister of Education we enjoyed the luxury of first class travel on the train. Once we reached New Delhi, his daughter Laila showed me all the historic places there and we made a trip to Agra to see the Taj Mahal and the Kutub Minar. Finally, college beckoned again and I boarded a train to Amritsar and then another for Lahore.

Back home, and although we were still only friends, I presented the ruby ring to Rasheda.

ENDNOTES

[i] I later went to Mahboob's Passing Out Parade at the

Pakistan Military Academy and cheered when my old school mate received the Sword of Honor.

[ii] Esso was the oil company that eventually became Exon.

3

On my last night In the hostel room I had lived in during my university days, I sat on my favorite spot – the windowsill.

Once when I was sitting on the windowsill a couple of years before with the full moon just above the tree tops, some little black specs were floating against it, perhaps some paper or leaves. Suddenly I had an idea for a story. I thought for a while and went to my study table and began to write.

The plot was simple: Space vehicles flying from the moon, some aliens had a base there and were leaving; they travelled to a large floating station where they disembarked onto an extended metal bridge like platform and entered a large vessel. Shortly after, there was a glow of multicolours and the station was gone. Soon it was approaching a whirlwind or whirlpool like opening like a hole in space; it was sucked in and appeared above a giant planet. The bridge was once again extended and all who were on board walked out to a waiting vehicle. As they sat comfortably in the transporter, it began to pull away from the mother ship. Someone said, "It's good to be home."

I called it *"Hole in Space." That was in 1958.* The story, four pages in all, it came into my head just after seeing those floating particles silhouetted against the moon. I read it and made a few corrections. Days later I submitted it to the editor of the college magazine "The Ravi" for the next issue. The editor had previously published several of my articles which were mainly on the humourous side.

Days later, I was summoned by the Principal. On his desk was "The Ravi." He picked it up and opened the page of my article. "What is this rubbish about a hole in space?" he asked and added, "How can there be a hole in empty space and for that matter a hole in thin air?"

I did not want to be disrespectful as he was my father's friend who had earlier at the time of joining the college, advised me to change my subject and prepare myself for the Civil Service Examination. "Sir," I said in a soft voice, "What I have written is just fiction. It is just an idea."

"Yes. Ideas are good, but there must be a limit," he told me and then using his fingers to make a circle he put his other hand through it. "See? The hand went through the circle, or hole as you call it, and nothing happened,"

I almost laughed, but instead I smiled. I couldn't believe what he was saying or doing. The Principal, had studied at Oxford University in the United Kingdom, and was a class mate of one of my uncles who was then a Cabinet Minister in India.

But he wasn't finished with me. "We are a prestigious institution, in fact, one of the top colleges not only in Pakistan but in the entire subcontinent. Some of India and Pakistan's great men graduated from here. We have to keep up that image, we can't have your kind of stuff."

I surrendered, made apologetic noises and left his office.

That night, sitting on the windowsill I thought back to the essay I had written in the Cambridge English Language Examination paper at school about a man riding a lion-like creature coming out of the lake. That essay earned me a Credit in the English Language paper. The Examiner must have appreciated my "imaginative" style. That story was more unusual than the "Hole in Space." The previous year I had failed in English. With this fiction essay I was rewarded and that made me think about the years I had spent climbing higher and higher. Later I heard a commotion. There seemed to be a serious argument. Some people spoke loudly but some laughed. Then I saw a few feet away from my window a student climbing down from a rope dangling from a drainage pipe. He could not pay his hostel fees and thought this was an easy way out. Unfortunately for him, hostel authorities waited on the ground. Later I was told that they became especially vigilant, especially after the examinations were completed.

During normal college days, the hostel main gates shut at 9:30 p.m. Some seniors used to sneak out by removing the large wire net windows in the toilets and replacing them on their return. Maybe my friend on the rope should have tried that trick.

After the commotion died down, I sat at my desk for several minutes, looking at the textbooks and notebooks I had filled in during the lectures. They had in a neat stack on a shelf and brought tears to my eyes. I would never see or touch them again and I felt I was leaving a friend behind. I wondered how I would get on in the "real" world where men and women dashed around as they ran the government, military and businesses. Where would I fit in?

A knock on the door of my cubicle snapped me out of contemplation. It was Sultan, a friend I'd shared a dormitory with since being admitted to the Seniors College Hostel. His hobby was painting and he was good at it. He painted a variety of subjects and earned some money from selling them. His interpretation of a stanza from Khalil Gibran's *The Prophet* was a masterpiece.

He was a solitary person with few words, spending most of his time with his brushes and canvases. A few months before I had given him a photograph of Rasheda telling him that I could not pay for it but asking if he would do a painting when he had nothing else to do. Without saying anything, he put it into his pocket. Four days later he presented me with a painting. It looked better than the photograph and in appreciation I took him out to dinner that night.

Sultan came from the Frontier Region of Pakistan and I met him some years later when I was posted to Chittagong. He was the Deputy Commissioner of the Hill Tracks. That was the last time I met him hut, as the saying goes, once a friend, always a friend.

I enjoyed my hostel days. I never knew what would happen, whom I would meet, or what would set me thinking.

Once, a few months earlier, the newspapers had articles about sending a man to the moon. When I was getting my hair cut, the barber asked me, "What happens if the moon sets before the man reaches it?" I almost jumped out of my seat and hid a smile until it almost developed into a burst of laughter. Somehow I controlled myself and just nodded with a deep hum. Then he added, "And to put their feet onto the holy grounds of the moon, that is sacrilege."

In the Muslim world the moon is considered "holy" as it tells the beginning and ending of the Lunar months and thus when to start fasting and when to end it. Not to get into an argument with my barber I added, "Of course, they must wear clean shoes."

My relationship with Rasheda was firm with commitments from both sides. We had not met or been in contact since the last days in the university. There was no way of meeting. Just getting in touch was difficult.

The day I left the hostel I contacted her on the phone. It was an effort because I feared that any of her eight brothers and sisters, much less her parents, would pick up the phone. One of her brothers, Iqbal, was junior to me at the college. We were friends and he knew of my relationship with his sister, so if anyone other than Rasheda answered my phone call, I could say I was phoning him. Luckily Rasheda picked up the phone and we chatted for some time and I told her my plans.

After leaving the hostel, I stayed a few days with my father's friend whom I had visited often. He was a Judge on the Pakistan Supreme Court. I enjoyed my visits to his home as he and his wife were like parents to me. Their son Sikander and daughter Sheerin were close friends.

On the day of departure from Lahore, Sikander took me to the airport to catch the flight to Dkaha where my father had settled after retirement. We were late; the flight had taken off minutes before. The next flight was the following day and before returning to his house, I asked him to drive me to Rasheda's house. He too knew about the relationship. When we reached the house, we asked for Iqbal. He hospitably arranged for some tea and sandwiches and then Rasheda appeared for a short while and we chatted discreetly just in case the watchful eye of her mother monitored us.

The next day I left for East Pakistan for the second time. The first had been in 1958 as a tourist. Now I was to stay.

My father had just retired from the diplomatic service and moved over to Dhaka where some of his brothers were posted. He now had to live on his meager pension and could barely look after his family. I blame him for his lack of foresight. He never took advantage of government offers of discounted land to staff, nor did he envision the day he retired and would need a home. He lived in a world where his job would be there forever. It's sad, but that's who he was.

On the other hand, my mother was more far-sighted. While posted in Iraq, she wanted to invest in real estate but my father had vetoed it. This was another example of his bad advice. However, he had many good points. He was a patriot and loved his country. He was always upright in the way he dealt with his fellow Pakistanis. He gave no one special treatment.

In Iraq one afternoon there had been a commotion in the front garden of our house. I rushed out and what hundreds of pieces of gold coins. A cooking pot was in the middle of them. I had never before seen my father so angry. A man had tried to bribe him with the gold coins. He called in the security guards to pick up the scattered coins and put them back into the pot, threatening to call the police in to charge him with attempted bribery.

The man fell at his feet and begged for mercy. In seconds my father was so cool you would think that nothing had happened. He let the man go with his gold. Later he found that the man was wanted by the police and needed a passport to leave Iraq. What a price – one cooking pot of gold for one passport. But I deeply respect my father for not taking that bribe.

Earlier he'd had many chances to enrich himself after the partition of the subcontinent. He was stationed then in Bombay/Mumbai when millions from both sides of the border moved one way or the other. A corrupt person could have made millions of rupees and retired. Today, in developing countries, it is rare to find a man with my father's integrity.

As I've said, retirement was never a topic my father

thought about. After his transfer to Iraq in 1952, his meager income barely covered our school fees and he couldn't afford the luxury of purchasing land, even at the low prices the government offered. His diplomatic income was just enough to keep him going. There were no extras. So after retirement, he came face to face with the reality that his government pension was negligible.

In Dhaka, my father was like a fish out of water. He'd been posted to Jeddah when he was only twenty-six and, upon his retirement at the age of fifty-eight, he seemed a foreigner in the land of his birth. For most of his life he had lived in mainly Arabic lands and experienced many cultures. It was worse for my mother who was an Arab from Saudi Arabia. I, as well, had landed in East Pakistan with no knowledge of the Bengali language. But I gained the highest educational achievements the country had to offer and I thank my parents for that.

To supplement their income, my mother put her business mind to work and started a little business of her own. She loved cooking and could produce tasteful dishes at short notice. She decided to produce tomato ketchup with the aid of a young servant boy who did her purchasing and found a way to procure empty bottles with screw caps. More importantly, he also found shops and little restaurants that purchased the home made product. My mother worked hard in her kitchen and enjoyed every moment of it. Money came in and augmented the pension.

Her cooking interest had begun after my father began attending formal dinners hosted by the British ambassador or his senior officials. He targeted food he particularly liked and discreetly placed them in an already prepared napkin in his pocket. Once he came home, my mother studied the sample and reproduced it the next day. My father loved his food and my mother spoiled him.

My father's last posting was Iraq. The photo below shows him and my mother with King Faisal and the Crown Prince Abdul Illah.

My father's general health until his retirement had been good for his age. He was active and wanted to do things. After a year in his retirement, he met with the then Pakistan Foreign Minister who was his friend for many years and was promised him an ambassadorial position to Kuwait. My mother was the happiest woman in the world as she would have been back to an Arabic speaking country.

A few days later the Foreign Minister called my father to have lunch with him at his residence in Dhaka. On arrival, my father was horrified to see an ambulance with attendants rushing around and his friend being carried out on a stretcher. That evening the news announced the sudden demise of the Foreign Minister due to a severe heart attack. That was the end of my father's hopes as the new minister appointed a man of his choosing.

Perhaps that sudden shock began to creep into his system and erode him from the inside. Diabetes came first, followed by depression. My mother insisted on their leaving Pakistan and returning to Saudi Arabia her home country. At that time she thought she had a home. Her parents' property offered enough accommodation for them. But when they landed in Saudi Arabia they got a most unwelcoming attitude from her one and only brother. She had looked forward to meeting him and his family after nearly sixteen years. Before her departure for Pakistan in 1949, she had arranged his marriage as she didn't want to leave him behind as a bachelor.

He was not pleased to see her and my father. He literally told her that she had no right to occupy any of the apartments of the houses they owned. Ultimately after hours of argument, her brother agreed to allow them to stay in one until they find alternative accommodation. On the ground floor of the house there were two sections. He gave them the smaller of the two. They were uncomfortable but they had no choice. Her brother had changed into a monster.

Some of her childhood friends visited regularly and spent many hours bringing her up to date with who is where and so on. She thus learned that her brother had sold some of the properties some time ago. Beside the four buildings, the family had some other properties owned by their parents. He had sold them and pocketed the money. Her brother was an employee of the government and had somehow manipulated the inheritance rights in such a way that she got nothing. When she confronted him, he showed her a document that stated that only males inherited property, not females. In the Islamic law the son and daughter inherit their parent's property and whatever they possessed in certain proportions. In this case he had completely erased her from the property inheritance document. Perhaps he thought that he'd never see her again.

My mother was a strong willed person and was ready for a fight, for her rights. She did not take it lying down. Days later she was at the Commissioner's office. He was sympathetic with her and ordered an enquiry. Her brother tried for some time to dilly-dally to avoid direct confrontation with the authorities. My mother's action prompted him to try to evict her from the premises. He failed.

Finally when the authorities could not challenge the inheritance document, for some unknown reason, they passed a judgment that my mother and her husband had to be given a full section in one of the buildings where she would live as long she and her husband were alive. What happened to the Islamic "Sharia" law? I do not understand my mother's situation and I can only hope that one day an honest and just person will explain it to me!

All that tension which lasted for months began to show on my father. He was a man of peace and seeing injustice done by his brother in-law and then the authorities giving a blind eye to my mother's rights began to affect his health. At the end my parents accepted the inevitable and found peace and lived comfortably. But at the back of their minds, the unfortunate situation that remained unsettled had a toll on their psyche and my father's failing health.

I didn't know about it at the time. Only when I came to visit my mother in 1972 did she tell me the whole story.

The night he passed away, he asked her to make fish cutlets, a favorite dish, then he watched television and enjoyed a plate of dry fruit. That was his last meal. He went to bed at midnight and during the night suffered a breathing problem. According to my mother, he sat up and once stood up on the bed, trying to breath with his hand in the air. Then he somehow felt comfortable and went to sleep. She woke up at seven in the morning, decided to let him sleep a little more, and after breakfast was ready, she went to wake him up. There was no response and after trying to shake him awake, she felt his cold stiff body. A doctor, hastily called him, told her, "It's too late. He must have died a few hours ago in his sleep."

He was buried in the *Umana Hawa* graveyard (the Mother Eve graveyard) back in Jeddah, near to the place he had spent those weeks in isolation after arriving there with chicken pox. All the tensions and stress he had gone through, the development of adult-diabetes through overeating, his high cholesterol and blood pressure ultimately resulted in partial paralysis on one side of his body and his death. He was only sixty-seven when he passed away on June 12, 1969—ironically, his own father died on the exact same day in 1951.

My father was a man out of time and place. He lived when money and tangible expressions of it determined success. In a time that prized honor and integrity above all else, he would have been revered.

My education was over. I had completed school, college and university at an almost record pace of twelve years dating from the day I sat in kindergarten class at Marie Colaco as an eleven year old. I had worked hard since that moment to the time I graduated with my Master's degree. I suppose I deserve to feel proud about my success. I am so grateful to my mother who fought so vigorously to give me the chance. She had pushed my father out of an underdeveloped Saudi Arabia in the 1940s with its archaic lifestyle, negligible opportunities for jobs other than those in the pilgrim industry, such as running a tea shop. Because, and only because of her, my sister Latifa

and I were exposed to a proper educational curriculum in Pakistan.

After receiving her B.A., Latifa went to the U.K. where she obtained her Master's degree in Journalism shortly after she had married Salim Kabir Sheikh, a graduate of Lincoln's Inn. Their daughter Saira, a barrister, recently became a QC. The second daughter

Shazia is a design architect and the son, Anwar, the youngest, is a senior banker.

As for me, my education seemed a vertical climb. I was always determined to reach the top, whatever it took. My personal roll of honor included achievements in sport (such as best sportsman of the year), leadership (the University Union, for example) and academics.

But, as always, there was a huge element of chance. What if my first attempt to pass the Cambridge Overseas School Certificate examination had been successful? I would not have sat across from those two girls and may never have met Rasheda, the love of my life. Rasheda, as well, had repeated a year in school, otherwise she would not have sat across from me. If she had not repeated that class and I had passed the exam on my first try we would not have met and our lives would have been so very different.

How do I summarize this? Was it destiny, coincidence, or the fulfillment of "what is written"? Whatever, the result was my heart's desire. It was the perfect ending to an uncertain childhood. A chapter in my life had come to a close.

The year was 1961.

Once I gained my Master's degree, I took a job as a lecturer at the Holy Cross College for Girls in Dhaka in East Pakistan. I had not given up on the Foreign Service but the next examination was months away. In the meantime, I decided to apply for a job with two commercial firms. One responded promptly, inviting me to an interview, and shortly afterwards I received an offer of employment as a senior executive by the Burmah-Shell Oil Storage and Distribution Company. There was a probationary period of two years during which I had to familiarize myself with the oil products, distribution networks, field marketing and sales covering aviation, bunkering, power houses and related services. My mother-in-law must have prayed hard for this opportunity with an oil company.

LOOKING THROUGH A KEYHOLE

4

My first two years with Burmah-Shell were a probationary period during which my training was directed to marketing petroleum products.

I started by learning how to clean and repair oil barrels, how to clean the large storage tanks and extinguish oil fires. I was one of six probationers and all of us came from rich and prestigious parents in senior government and military services.

We were shown no mercy. After a month we were posted to different locations. I was sent to the aviation section at the Airport where I learned how to fuel aircrafts and everything associated with that process and then I was off to another location in the countryside to be with local distributors in villages and little towns. In one location I lived in a makeshift mud hut where there was no toilet. I was told to pick up two bricks and go to the field. One week there was like eternity. Not surprisingly two of our probationer colleagues dropped out during this period. They could not adjust.

Finally I was posted to Lahore Divisional Office and that was a heavenly change. I was then in the city where Rasheda lived and I kept in touch with her on daily basis. But after a few months later I was reassigned to East Pakistan to familiarize me with that part of the country.

While in Dhaka I received the sad news that my friend Sikandar had died in a car crash on his way back from his honeymoon in Afghanistan. He had been driving on the Khyber Pass road when he had unsuccessfully tried to avoid an oncoming speeding truck. His car fell hundreds of feet killing them instantly. In those days the Pakistan Frontier Region and Afghanistan offered many holiday spots and tourists moved freely without any worry or difficulty. Today those areas are a war zone!

Alas!

With only a few months left in my probationary period, Rasheda began to pressure me to get married. I wanted to wait till after my confirmation in my job. So far my parents had no idea of our affair. Finally, I told my mother and showed her a picture of Rasheda. She approved of her: "If that is what you want, I have no objection. I will talk to your father."

But, my father told her that he had been approached by his brother in the police, the husband of Auntie Tahira, who had proposed his daughter for me. It was an embarrassing situation for me as Auntie Tahira had been affectionate and caring. Had we known about the plan much earlier the situation would have been different. My father also revealed that other prominent Bengali families had proposed marriage and that some had even hinted at pushing my career forward. It was the usual thing. Girls whose parents had influential connections with X or Y or those with rich families promising a more luxurious living was the accepted way of life. Families looked for their sons or daughters to further their social interests.

As far as I was concerned, I didn't need any of that. I was already in one of the country's most prestigious companies as a senior executive with a brilliant future. There, promotion came only through hard work. No outside push was required and, as far as living facilities, the best was provided. I had achieved the best that one needs on my own merit.

I explained all of this to my father and mother and, using his antiquated typewriter from the early 1920s, he wrote a proposal of marriage and sent it to Rasheda's father. (Speaking of his typewriter, he always claimed that while working in the British Legation in the early 1930s he received a package with his name on it. When he opened it, it was a typewriter. He returned it to the Legation saying he had not ordered one. But they insisted that as it was addressed to him, he must accept it. He never knew who the sender was.)

Rasheda must have done her part with her parents and soon there was a reply of acceptance. Her parents visited my parents in Dhaka and a date was fixed.

But there was a problem. Technically I could not marry until I completed my executive probationary period. However, I took a chance and wrote to my Dhaka Divisional Manager, Michael Cooke. A little push was also required by Rasheda's father Dr. Abdul Aziz Khan FRCS, Principal of Fatima Jinnah Medical College and Sir Ganga Ram Hospital was known by his own right to most prominent people in Pakistan. The Deputy General Manager of Burmah – Shell, Mr. A.R. Faridi, just happened to be his friend from pre-partition days of the Sub Continent. Soon the approval came as a "special case" and the wedding was arranged for the 24th of April, 1964.

Only one day's leave was granted, a Friday before the week end. My parents and I flew to Lahore, where we were joined by Akbar Uncle, my father's brother, and Wasi Uncle who were posted in West Pakistan. Akbar Uncle signed our document of marriage. Some of my friends who were with me at Burn Hall School were invited and, to my surprise I saw them marching into the ceremony with my school's Principal of Burn Hall, Father J. Klaver![i] I was so happy to see him. Thanks to my schoolmate Mr. Zafar Qureshi who brought him all the way from Abbottabad — about three hundred miles away.

By 9 p.m. the ceremony was over and my bride Rasheda and I left for her parents' newly constructed and unoccupied house in Gulberg, a newly developed part of Lahore. We spent the night there together with my parents and guests. The next day we flew back to Dhaka accompanied by Nadra, Rasheda's younger sister.

At the Dhaka Airport my father's other brother Alamgir Uncle the Inspector General of Police and Auntie Tahira met us at the aircraft and took us straight to the VIP lounge which was jammed with relatives, friends and some of my students from Holy Cross College. My uncle's chauffer driven car was decorated with strings of flowers; Then Rasheda and I sat like VIPs in my uncle's chauffer-driven car and drove home.

The next day was a Sunday. My uncle Alamgir

arranged a grand "Walima" or a dinner reception at his residence where all friends and relatives, the former Governor General and later the Prime Minister of Pakistan, the Governor of East Pakistan Province and some senior businessmen attended. The photo below shows my father and Alamgir Uncle greeting the governor.

The following day I was in office, back to work. What a letdown. All that wedding activity in just three days, Friday, Saturday and Sunday.

A few months later I was transferred back to Karachi for the final days of my probationary period. One morning I was summoned to the main office to meet the General Manager of Burmah-Shell. Another probationer was in the waiting room and we found out that out only we two had managed to complete the training period. I must add that it was not an easy task as shown by the dropout rate.

The secretary took me into the General Manger's large office. A tall well-dressed gentleman got up from his desk and walked over to greet me and then took me to an adjoining room that was a lounge for special visitors. He sat in chair next to me and his secretary asked, "What would you like to drink, hard or soft?"

At first I did not understand her question. My host seeing my confused expression put me at ease. "I am having some gin and tonic. How about you?" Gin and tonic were foreign words to me. Neither my father nor most of the family drank alcohol so, consequently, I was unfamiliar with the names for alcoholic beverages.

I didn't know what gin or tonic meant but as my host seemed to suggest it was a good thing, I confidently told the secretary, "Thank you. I will have the same." It was a total shot in the dark. After the drinks were served, the secretary walked up to a desk and returned with a box of cigars. The General Manager took the box and extended his hand in offer.

"Mr. Kabir, congratulations. You have done excellently and you are confirmed as a Senior Executive Assistant. Welcome to Burmah-Shell. Let's have a cigar to celebrate this occasion." His words were like an angel telling me that I had earned a place in Heaven! His secretary trimmed one end of the cigar and lit it for me. After a few puffs and a sip of gin and tonic I was in a different world.

Beginning with casual talk, the General Manager gradually drifted to the responsibilities of an executive, ending with, "In a commercial organization like Burmah-Shell, the staff are paid well and looked after. At the end of our careers we don't expect to be rich people, but we'll be comfortable." Those words meant a lot.

After we finished our drinks and smoked just a few puffs of my cigar he got up and put his hands on my shoulder and walked me to the door. His last words were, "I am confident you will do well Good luck."

Cigar in hand I walked to my waiting colleague, "Congratulations in advance," I said to him as he was the next for the ritual.

During the probationary period, the company arranged my accommodation in a hotel not too far from the office in Karachi. That hotel had been the home of all probationers for decades. An old building with single rooms, a bachelor set up, with a few bigger rooms for married couples. I was in one of them.

It was perhaps built a century ago and close to railway tracks that ran along side of it. Its name, North Western Hotel, perhaps related to the North Western Railways when it must have been used to accommodate expatriates in the old days. The owner at the time was a very sophisticated entrepreneur. He had a small restaurant tucked in one corner of the building called Agha's Tavern'

That night to celebrate my "confirmation as a senior executive," Rasheda and I decided to celebrate. When we entered the Tavern the man at the door stopped us. "You must have a tie to enter" From a box on the reception desk he plucked a tie readied for undressed clients and helped me to put it on. Inside the atmosphere were serene, dim lights, soft classical music playing in the background; there were only seven tables and a bar. A waiter seated us at one corner. The food was superb, far different from what we were having from hotel service in our room.

I was then transferred to East Pakistan, where we were housed by the Company in a grand and luxurious two-story apartment house. A newly employed Bengali gentleman who had worked with Boeing in the United States occupied the lower flat. We enjoyed each other's company. He had a daughter just month older than our Shahnaz.

A war with India broke the peace and tranquility in both the wings of Pakistan in 1965. It was over Kashmir, a dispute since the Partition of the Indian Sub Continent in August 1947 formed Bharat, or India, and the newly created state of Pakistan. The rulers of Kashmir opted for India though the majority of the people was Muslims and wanted to be with Pakistan. In 1948 both countries went to war. The United Nations intervened and a ceasefire resulted with the *Line of*

Control. Each side kept the areas occupied during the war but there was no final solution and soon peace was restored with no winners.

Burmah-Shell, for whatever reason, decided to sell its Shell part to the Burmah Oil Company, its partner, and transferred some of the Burmah-Shell executives to the newly formed Burmah Eastern Ltd. Included in this arrangement were our East Pakistan Divisional Manager, my neighbor living below me, two others and myself because the Burmah Oil Company had no marketing or operational staff. It was mainly a storage facility and it distributed petroleum products to marketing Companies like Burmah-Shell, Esso and Caltex. Hence the necessity to bring in and absorb some professionals.

The Main Office was in Chittagong, a port city so we had to move – once again.

I did not want to go.

5

Chittagong[i] is magnificent–both then and now. It extends deep into the Hill Tracks and down to the beautiful beaches of Cox's Bazaar. The Karnaphuli River meanders along its southern boundary before emptying into the Bay of Bengal and undulating roads link homes on countless outcrops and merge old and new together. In 1971, the managers of foreign and local companies, senior executives, and businessmen knew each other intimately and met every weekend at the only club, The Chittagong. Mostly they huddled around its famous bar.

By now I had married Rasheda and been blessed with my daughter Shahnaz.

My family and I toured most of the area with friends, driving up into the hills to Rangamati Lake and beyond, enjoying meals with the tribal Raja of the Hill Tracks. Once Rasheda and I ventured deeper into the Hill Tracks where pigmy-like people lived on stilted thatched huts few feet above the ground. They were short, fair in complexion and almost naked with beads and old colonial coins as decorative ornaments around their neck and waists.

Once we visited a hut and I saw a young boy in his teens carving something from a bamboo shoot. Then, he picked up a flute lying next to him that he had made earlier and played for us. The tune was so haunting and magical that I wished we had the time to spend with his people and learn more about their music and what it said. Mingling with that tribe and the walk in the forest reminded me of Sir Arthur Conan Doyle's "The Lost World." Of course, there were no dinosaurs or apelike people; but the general scenario gave the impression of prehistoric life style. It was fun and educative.

I spent six years in Chittagong and they were the best period in my life.

Chittagong is my city. I loved it—its appearance and its way of life and its grand historical background that rivals some of the oldest civilizations.[ii] It was where I expected to live for a very long time, maybe forever, and that is why the events of March 1971 hit so hard and hurt so much.

For a better understanding of those events, it is necessary to know the area's recent history. Up to 1947 India and the Pakistans were one country, part of the British Empire, with King George VI as Emperor. Then largely due to the leadership of Mahatma Gandhi, India gained independence as a sovereign state. The largely Islamic Dominion of Pakistan was also created. Initially part of the British Commonwealth with King George VI as king, it became a republic in 1956 and remained largely under martial law in 1970 when democratic elections were held amid bitter and divisive political fighting. Unfortunately it was geographically divided into West Pakistan and East Pakistan. West Pakistan housed the government and was bordered on the west by Afghanistan and Iran, Kashmir to the north, the Arabian Sea and India to its west and east. The smaller and relatively less powerful East Pakistan had India to its west, Bhutan on its north, the Bay of Bengal to the south and Burma to its east. There was a large economic disparity between the Pakistan and it was particularly galling that West Pakistan with a lower population was far more affluent than that of its eastern counterpart. Both Pakistans were suspicious of each other and the Bengalis in East Pakistan were restless and resentful.

A crisis ensued after the Bengali nationalist leader, Sheikh Mujibur Rahman's Awami League won a landslide victory in the 1970 national elections. Thus he had the constitutional right to form a government and become Prime Minister of both sections. However, Mr. Bhutto of West Pakistan refused to acknowledge this. Instead he proposed two prime ministers: one for East Pakistan, the other for the west. East Pakistan reacted to the idea with outrage. Again the less populous west was dictating to it.

Early in 1971 the Bengali nationalist leader, Sheikh Mujibur Rahman met with President Yahya Khan and the West Pakistan leader of the Pakistan People's Party Zulfikar Ali Bhutto to "solve" the political impasse and perhaps the fate of the country. Afterwards Rahman said that he would continue to dialogue for a settlement of the crises. In reality, perhaps the talks had already failed with Bhutto and Khan leaving East

Pakistan empty handed, although maybe something was cooked that satisfied both sides.

On March 7, 1971 Rahman hinted that there would be consequences such as secession if his demands were not met and asked the East Pakistanis to struggle for freedom and independence. In response the government appointed a general as governor of East Pakistan, flew in thousands of troops and despatched warships carrying ammunition and more soldiers.

Rahman's speech a couple of days later had no threatening words, but all the ingredients of an unhappy man who wanted what the majority of his people had chosen—his right to become the nation's elected Prime Minister. He sensed that Khan's armed response to the talks was the last straw and that he guessed what was coming. What added even more fuel to the fire was the sudden crackdown of the army on local police, universities and the intellectual elite, for only then Rahman signed a declaration of independence[iii] and declared that he would fight the West Pakistani army. He was arrested that night.

Sheikh Mujib's speech ignited East Pakistan. The public became hostile to the authorities and rebellious. In Chittagong some people were killed during a political rally. Although these were writings on the wall, I was still not willing to come to terms with or face the reality that would come. Maybe a refusal to look into the future and face facts ran in the family.

My friend Mac, a Freemason, and my brother from

the same Lodge busted my cocoon by telling me we had to leave East Pakistan immediately. "East Pakistan is hurtling towards a civil war. Families must leave. We are advising all our close friends to leave and offering assistance."

"But I can't go."

Before I could finish my sentence he interrupted. "You can stay, but your family must leave. I can arrange air transportation from Dhaka to Karachi. You must make your own arrangements to send them by train to Dhaka." He paused, then added quickly, "How many tickets do you need?"

The whole affair was too sudden. However, I thought quickly. "Two for my wife and daughter, three for my sister and her two daughters,[iv] plus one for the maid. Altogether, six."

Mac was silent for a moment. "I will give you nine tickets, just in case you need to give them to friends." Before I could say anything, he got up to leave. "Okay. Your nine tickets will be here by tomorrow."

He left, and I got the impression that either he didn't want to say anything or that he couldn't. Later I came to know that getting airline tickets was next to impossible. Industrialists and businessmen offered factories and fortunes for tickets from Dhaka to Karachi in their desperation to get their families out of East Pakistan. Through Mac, though, we had VIP treatment and he arrived back the next day with the promised nine tickets.

"How much do I owe?" I asked, prepared to pay almost anything.

"We'll talk about that later. Just arrange to have them on their flight the day after tomorrow."

"Mac, thank you. Thank you very much for your help..."

Before I could finish the sentence, he interrupted. "Just let us have a drink. We will talk about all this after their safe journey."

It could not have been a happier moment for me than to enjoy a drink with him. It was just like normal times when life was free from worrying thoughts.

Mac had just forced me to face one reality but I knew there was much more to know. He would not have acted the way he did, giving us tickets so promptly, unless he knew something. He was a senior member of a large British firm and, being so, had access to many sources of information, maybe even diplomatic ones.

That night I called Rafi, a Bengali friend, and told him that my wife and daughter and my sister must leave for Dhaka to catch a flight to Karachi in two days. Half an hour later he and his wife were in our house. Without hesitation he offered to make all the train arrangements and, on top of that, to accompany them. True to his word, he arrived back at the house at ten the next morning, March 11, 1971. We drove to the railway station and in minutes my wife and daughter, my sister Latifa and her daughters Saira and Shazia, our maid together with two other women, close friends of my wife. She had given them two of the extra tickets and kept one back in case my sister's husband in Dhaka would need it.

As the train blared its intention to leave, Rafi extended his hands through the compartment window and shouted, "Don't worry. They are safe with me. I will deliver them to your uncle's home and will see you on my return."

I stood on the platform until the train disappeared from sight thinking, *They are safe with Rafi. He is a good friend. He will see to their safety.* Comforted by my thoughts, I returned home late in the afternoon. The house was empty. There were no sounds of activity, no cries from children. There was pin drop silence. I switched the radio on and fiddled with the dial trying to find any news but there was nothing of interest on the Pakistani stations. Sometimes I told myself that the situation was serious. At other times I thought that it was possible that nothing would happen.

I fretted about my family. They were scheduled to arrive in Dhaka early the next day. I tried to while away the time by talking with friends, listening to news broadcasts from the BBC, Radio Pakistan and VOA (Voice of America) but none said anything about East Pakistan. I dozed off, wondering if perhaps I had overreacted.

The phone rang about 2 p.m. the next day. My uncle in Dhaka said, "Rasheda is here. Talk to her." My Akbar Uncle's voice was calm and reassuring. Later that night he called again to confirm their departure. He had personally escorted them to the plane.[v]

My relief was immeasurable, especially after rumors reported that the Chittagong-Dhaka train that day, also packed with West Pakistanis, was attacked by Bengali students and other miscreants who brutally killed and inhumanely tortured men, women and children. Only God knows if this was true, but it is what I heard and believed in Chittagong.

Alone with my house boy and the cook I told myself, “There is nothing to worry about. Not now.” I went to the office as on any other day but, a few days after my family had left East Pakistan, the new general manager, who replaced my colleague a couple of months earlier, called me to his office.

He was a Bengali who had lived in the United Kingdom and worked with the Burmah Oil Company for some years. His attitude and behavior to the staff was that of superiority. As the general gossip in the office had it, he was more British than the British. Employees called him, (with due apology), *Kala Angraise* or black Englishman.[vi] After a polite exchange of words he put a question so bluntly that I wondered if I was being interrogated for a crime, “I understand you have sent your family out of East Pakistan.” Before I could answer, he added, “Why?” His tone showed the unacceptability of my decision to send my family away.

For a moment I could not comprehend what he was

driving at. Then he added, "You know what people would think. It was not a good decision."

I was still confused as to what crime had been committed by sending my family out of East Pakistan. "Ashif," I said, calling him by his first name. "My wife has gone to Lahore on many occasions in the past. Sometimes twice a year. Her parents are there. What is so wrong now that she has left?"

"Well, the timing is wrong. We are in a political crisis. Being a Bengali Company, we should not attract attention because our staff are fleeing."

I interrupted him. "Ashif, what are you talking about? What has her travelling got to do with political crises?" I paused. He was irritating. The best way to handle him was to respond bluntly and that is what I did. "What I did with my family is a personal matter. It has nothing to do with the Company or anyone else. My family come and go as they please."

Being a Bengali upstart, Ashif had been promoted to the post of General Manager from a rather lowly position in the Burmah Oil Company management ladder. This was primarily due to the political decision to have a Bengali in charge rather than an Englishman or any other nationality. When he realized that I was not taking the conversation lightly, he softened, "What I tried to tell you earlier before you interrupted me is that the timing was wrong. You know people misunderstand what you have done. Being a member of the senior staff, it does not give a good impression."

As I didn't interrupt he rolled on, "You see, we are a Bengali Company, and our staff must behave like one. Sending your family to West Pakistan gives the wrong impression that our senior staff are overreacting to the situation here, as if they are afraid that the Bengalis will misbehave with the West Pakistanis and ...."

I cut him off. I was not in a pleasant mood, "Whatever you are trying to tell me, does not make sense. In any case whatever I decide for my family has got nothing to do with you or what the general public thinks. As you know I am due for my annual leave next month and, as always, I send my wife in advance to have more time with her family. You are unnecessarily reacting." I paused, and before he could open his mouth, continued firmly, "Ashif, you just run the company and let me run my life."

Perhaps he couldn't believe his ears. He was silent and played with a pencil. "Is that all, or is there another matter to discuss?" I asked and walked to the door. He did not speak. He was perhaps shocked by one of his staff answering him in that fashion. Being a *Kala Angraize* he expected that we, the subordinates, would not answer him back. Our former General Manager, a Brit, never ever displayed such antics in words or action. We were colleagues and on first person basis.

The following days ran smoothly with no strikes or political disturbances. It was business as usual. We partied and the Chittagong Club resumed its pleasures. On the surface it looked like that everything was getting back to normal. Neither we nor the general public had the slightest hint of what was to come. Serious political trouble was brewing and the Pakistani authorities kept a watchful eye. The secessionists were set to come out into the open and start a civil war.

That was when the bubble burst on the 25th of March and the Pakistani Army displayed its might against activists and supporters and secessionist sympathisers. No mercy was shown by either side.

The so-called treason against the State of Pakistan was being committed by a political party. Military action of that scale was perhaps unjustified. The leaders could have been taken to have a dialogue as political talks were then called. They were not criminals but politicians who wanted a just solution for the betterment of their province. But the government perhaps felt it was too late for such niceties. With the mood throughout the province favoring independence, perhaps it really was too late for across the table talks. Even if Sheikh Mujib was offered the position of Prime Minister of Pakistan he may have refused it. There was no turning back. It was too late.

People talk. Someone told me that as the two major political parties never saw eye to eye, there could never have been a compromise. And, while that was clearly understood by the elite of Pakistan, few perhaps realized that for the situation to reach such a level it had tailored so by a handful of personalities. If that was the plot, then all the actors committed treason and allowed gruesome atrocities to justify their means to an end.

Was it necessary to sacrifice hundreds of thousands of innocent lives? History tells us yes. People throughout time have sacrificed their lives for justice, equality and freedom. The story of Bangladesh is merely another page to be added to the books.

It is a great pity however, that two great cultures who had found a common goal to strive to shine in the sun together had sadly felt it was not meant to be. With a tinge of humor let me add that is how the ball bounces. For me, an ignorant outsider, not knowing the ins and outs of this vast political theater of dos and don'ts, it was like "looking through a keyhole" into a vast room with only that small orientation to formulate my view.

Was Rudyard Kipling's interpretation of "East is East, and West is West, and the twain shall never meet"[vii] correct? It certainly seems to apply to different cultures of people whether they are Eastern or Western who don't see eye to eye and some use it as an excuse for their actions.

In 1971 we would have done well, however, to have reflected on the last lines of that poem where Kipling implies that if two protagonists with ability and courage stand face to face barriers might not exist.

ENDNOTES

[i] Chittagong is the home and birthplace of revered Buddhists and great kings. According to one story, more than six hundred years ago a Muslim preacher Hazrat Badar Aawlia arrived in the city from overseas and chose Cheragi Pahar as his vantage point to spread the message of Islam among the locals. It was at the top of this hill that the pious messenger lit a "chati" (lamp) and called out "azaan" the call for prayer to the people to join him in prayer. Chittagong's name can then be traced unmistakably back to the "chati." and the suffix "gaon" meaning village, became "Chatigaon." Another theory is that the first group of Kulin Brahmins to have settled in this region (after it was incorporated into Bengal from the Arakanese were 'chatt-upadhyays'). Hence this region came to be known as chatto-gan, is the Bengali term for village. However, whatever is the true story, at least we have something to tell us how it got its name. It has been a seaport since a few centuries B.C. The Romans knew of it. Claudius Ptolemy called it one of the best ports in the eastern world. Trade with the Arab world began in the 9th Century AD, and during the sixteen century it became a hub for Portuguese trade. During the British rule, Chittagong made several attempts to gain independence, but failed.

[ii] Historically, Chittagong was ruled by the ancient kingdom of Arakan up to the 17th Century, albeit with

gaps. Sultan Fakruddin Mubarak Shah of Sonargaon conquered the city in 1340. A successor, Sultan Giasuddin Mubarak Shah, constructed a highway from Chittagong to Chandpur on the confluence of the Megna and Padma rivers and ordered the construction of many of Chittagong's lavish mosques and tombs. After the defeat of Mahmud Shah at the hands of Sher Shah in 1538, the Arakanese regained Chittagong. From this time onward, until its conquest by the Mughals, this region was under the control of the Portuguese and the Magh pirates. The Portuguese, during the era of their greatness in Asia, gained a temporary establishment in Arakan but, in 1784 the Burmese (now Myanmar) conquered the province.

Sonargaon is the ancient capital of Isa Khan's Kingdom in Bengal. It is located near the current-day city of Narayanganj, Bangladesh. It is the eastern terminus of the Grand Trunk Road, built by Sher Shah Suri in the 16th century, and which extends approximately 1500 miles across northern India and Pakistan up to Peshawar in the North West Province of West Pakistan. It is said that the famous Muslim traveler Ibn Battuta visited the city in the 14th century. Chittagong, which was part of Arakan, was invaded and occupied by the Mughal Empire in 1666. The Mughal Commander Shaista Khan and his son Umed Khan expelled the Arakanese from the area in 1666 and established Mughal rule. They renamed *Chittagong as Islamabad*.

[iii] A copy of the declaration eventually reached some students in Chittagong.

[iv] My sister and her two daughters were visiting us on a holiday. They had come from Lahore a week before while her husband was in Dhaka on business.

[v] As the sister's husband had already left Dhaka, the extra ticket went to the wife of the Pakistan Arline manager in Chittagong who had traveled with them on the train to Dhaka.

[vi] This terminology is common in the subcontinent for such persons, and no disrespect is intended.

[vii] From Rudyard Kipling's *The Ballad of East and West* first published in 1889. While the first line is often quoted, most people completely miss the third and fourth lines and their meaning:

But there is neither East nor West, Border, nor Breed, nor Birth,

When two strong men stand face to face, though they come from the ends of the earth!

6

It seemed a day like every other when I came home from my office on Thursday, 25 March 1971. I had an early dinner and went for my usual walk to the top of our hill[i] and back several times before sitting down on a little bench outside my house I lit a cigarette and looked down at the road below that skirted our hill and disappeared into darkness. The street lights were so dim that one could not see his own shadow. I saw only pitch darkness with a distant and faint light from hundreds of homes on the hills. Most had been built after the Independence of Pakistan to house senior staff such as businessmen, shipping companies' executives, railways staff, military personnel and the local elite. The dark sky above displayed its enormous wonders, exhibiting the countless stars. That night the Milky Way offered inspiration. Chittagong proposed darkness and apprehension and it felt like a lull before a storm.

There was an eerie silence. It was so strange with no cars, no people on the road. At this time, nine o'clock, the road was normally buzzing with activity. Lost in thought, I had no understanding of what would happen. I remembered my friend Mac's warning to leave Chittagong a few weeks earlier and wondered if he knew something he did not tell us.

A voice behind me interrupted my thoughts. "Can I join you?" asked my next door neighbor and added as he puffed on his pipe, "God knows what's going to happen tomorrow."

"Why? Is there going to be trouble? The strike will be as usual. They will march, create a lot of noise and the day after we'll go back to business as usual," I said confidently as I got up from my bench.

"No, my friend. This time it is more serious. There are reliable rumors that Sheikh Mujib will declare independence tomorrow." Then he added in a more positive tone, "Someone told me that Mujibur Rahman openly declared the secession of East Pakistan. God only knows what the true story is."

"Perhaps he said that to scare the opposition."

He handed me a glass of Scotch. "Here. Take this. It should wake you up."

The cubes of ice settled down as I shook the glass. I took a sip and lit a cigarette. My friend puffed his pipe and casually added, "Politics is a dirty business; there are no set rules, especially not in this part of the world. Bhutto will not allow Mujib to have the honor of becoming Prime Minister." He paused and had another long drag at his pipe. "Come. Let me show you something," he said and walked back to his house. I followed. Then he pointed to a red X crudely marked on the wall.

"What is that?" I asked.

"I am told by our Bengali friends who are for the unity of Pakistan that Mujib's guys used the telephone directory to pick out all who are West Pakistani and this X to identifies them. This is not a good sign. It's something to worry about."

At that moment it didn't make any sense to me.

"I think you are overreacting," I told him and began to walk back to the bench.

"Hasan, I believe these crosses identify the West Pakistanis and, if required, they will collect them and ship them back to West Pakistan. Or, perhaps," he added bluntly after a long pause, "perhaps they will butcher them."

"That is not a kind thing to say. We are not living in the dark ages."

"Yes, but when it comes to nationalism or sectarianism, history is full of it."

"I don't agree with you," I argued strongly. "Do you think the world will stand by and let such atrocities take place? *Never.*"

He puffed furiously on his pipe. "Yes, the world community will denounce such action, but it will be lip service only. Radio and television will say all they want and the big powers will show concern and offer false promises to prevent such an event..." Shams paused.

"The bottom line is what is *in* it for them? Is India involved in this conspiracy with Mujib? He will need them if the Pakistan army steps in to squash his rebellion, and we know that India is itching to weaken and destabilize Pakistan."

"But, Shams, there is no X on my house..."

Before I could finish what I had to say, he interrupted. "You work for a Bengali British company, as in the case of our other friends who are employees of foreign firms. They have no red Xs on their homes either. It is only us who are private businessmen or those working for West Pakistani companies who have them." He sighed deeply before adding, "Why is this hatred for us? We set up businesses and created jobs for millions of Bengalis. We've made this province our home."

I didn't know what to say but while I thought I tried to put him at ease. "Everything is possible. Logically, though, if the Bengalis want independence, why should they take their anger out on innocent civilians? They should fight it out with the authorities and, if they get what they want, they will need the trust of all those who have invested here to maintain the province's economic stability. It would be foolish of them to destroy it."

Shams shook his head. "Logically you may be right but for one reason or another they have some inner dislike or hatred for West Pakistanis. And for Punjabis particularly. Why? Are we more enterprising in commerce and agriculture? Historically Punjab has been the bread basket of the subcontinent. We have proven our mettle in all fields from military to commerce. We have earned an enviable position as a race, and that has trickled down to a number of communities who see it as a sign of dominance."

We talked and talked, theorizing possible scenarios, but I was not convinced that something drastic would happen. "It will not be all that bad as you look at it," I told Shams. "Bengal has an enviable history too. Its rich culture and contribution to the creation of Pakistan cannot be denied. In fact, Bengalis did more than the politicians of West Pakistan. Bengal's role goes back for several centuries. Some politicians have to get some history lessons. Bengalis are very established in the politics of the subcontinent.

He swirled the remaining Scotch. "I hope you are right." He sighed and emptied his glass in one large gulp. After a pause he suggested going to the Club. "We may hear something there."

It was nearly ten o'clock. For a moment I thought it was not a good idea. The empty roads did not look inviting. Before I could say anything, he walked towards his car. "Come on. Let's go." We left our glasses on the bonnet of his second car. "The boy will pick them up," he said and opened the car door.

I stood and thought for a moment. I was not comfortable with the idea. "Okay," I agreed finally. "Let's go for a short while."

Shams started the car and drove downhill to meet the main road. It was dead. Empty and deserted. Two hundred feet from the Club, two civilians dressed in the local white attire but with red armbands appeared from nowhere and waved their hands for us to stop. We rolled down our windows and before either of us could speak, one of them said gently in English, "Brothers, where are going?"

"To the Chittagong Club. Just over there," I said and pointed in its direction. Then I noticed several other men not far away holding spades and pickaxes.

"Don't stay late. Try to be home before midnight," their leader advised respectfully and waved for us to go on.

As we drove, Shams whispered, "I think they are going to dig the road up and perhaps all the roads in the city to stop vehicles moving."

What vehicle movements were they worried about? Did they want to stop police action against unruly strikers? Maybe Shams was right after all and something big would happen the next day. For the first time I felt uneasy.

When we reached the Club, the parking lot was empty. "There is no one here," I said after looking around.

"No, there is a car out there near the guard's room. Niazi's car, if I am not wrong."

"Good for us. He is a shipping man and well connected. Surely he will have better information and will enlighten us," I said as we walked towards the Club's staircase.

The Club was built on a plateau just about twenty feet above road level. At the top of the entrance a sprawling lawn greeted us and to our right there were several small well-manicured and colorfully painted villas for members' guests from outside the city. The Club's library offered books for varying tastes, mostly donated by members and friends when transferred from Chittagong to another location. Some books had signatures going back into the 1920s. The bar, usually an instant meeting place for business or refreshment, was an institution. Tonight it was a gloomy sight.

As Shams and I walked towards it, I looked at the lawns to my left. They were empty—no one there, no loud laughter, no friends exchanging jokes or eating favorite meals. Nothing. The tables with their white linen ready to welcome any guests sat empty as well.

How many unforgettable evenings had my wife and I enjoyed the dimly lit lawns as we relished fabulous meals from the Club's kitchen that rivalled any five star hotel. One occasion I remember to this day. Around midnight, while enjoying a meal with friends, out of nowhere and high above us, three large balls of fires streamed together faster than an aircraft or air force jet as they crossed the sky silently towards the Bay of Bengal.

"What was that?" someone asked.

"Perhaps they were some kind of UFO," I replied jokingly.

It was an unusual sight. The closest answer would be asteroids, but three of them in formation were unlikely. The memory of that event faded as Shams and I entered the bar and saw no one at first. Then a voice from the far end broke the silence with thunderous greetings. "Come and join us." Our friend raised his hand and beckoned us over.

We were glad to see Niazi. The shipping man sat with four men who looked European. Shams and I waved backed. "We'll join you. Let's get our drinks," Shams said as he looked at the bartender and showed two fingers. "Two Scotches. On the rocks."

The bar was designed, built and decorated with the best materials money could buy in the early twentieth century. The walls were laced with teakwood and the mirrors must have been imported. Busts of founding members and famous Bengali poets graced its shelves. A few gold-framed paints of British royalty (perhaps kept as a reminder of the "good old days") hung on the walls together with a few others depicting local scenic beauty.

As we waited for our drinks, my eye caught an inscription that was beautifully carved in gold letters on dark wood and had been contributed by one of the members—*No one dares bomb this club.* The wars with India had become a common feature, so to speak. The first, after Independence in 1948, was over Kashmir which both countries claimed. As it had a Muslim majority, rightfully it should have been allotted to Pakistan because the basic concept for the creation or partition of the subcontinent had been based on Muslim majority areas belonging to Pakistan. India and Pakistan did not see eye to eye about this heaven-like piece of earth called Kashmir. *Who had blundered when drawing the geographic boundaries? What was their motive?*

On the wall behind Niazi and his friends was my wife's first serious painting done after she had joined the Ladies Painting Club a few years earlier. She had some knowledge about using colors but no professional guidance. However, in a short time she produced good works of art. The painting on the teakwood wall represented late autumn in an imaginary forest with countless orange and crimson leaves, some carpeting the forest floor. A small stream meandered through a clearing. Perhaps the scene was somewhere in Canada. Rasheda was thrilled some thirty-five years later when a friend from Chittagong came to Saudi Arabia where we then lived and proudly told her that her painting still hung in the Club Bar. It had found its place among equals, among the old paintings that were part of the Club's history. Perhaps it was an epitaph of East Pakistan's final moments.

That night I looked at the sign above the bar and sadly said to myself, "I just hope that no one bombs this place." Then I picked up a plate of nuts and joined

Niazi and his friends. He introduced us. They were Yugoslav engineers working on a government project and staying at the Club. As their English was poor, we exchanged a few polite sentences. Shams was impatient and could wait for formalities to be completed and bluntly asked Niazi about the situation. "What do you think is going to happen tomorrow? Rumors say that Mujib will declare the secession of East Pakistan from Pakistan."

"Can't really think they will go to that extreme, but from what we hear about the result of that meeting with the General and Bhutto, Mujib was not too happy. Perhaps he will go to any length to..." He paused and then added strongly, "Or perhaps the three of them made a deal authored, of course, by Bhutto. He lowered his voice. "Bhutto will go to any length as long as he gets power. He can't see a Bengali becoming Prime Minister."

"But that is old news. What is going to happen tomorrow?" Shams was insistent. Perhaps driven by the red X, he wanted to hear more than speculations that everyone knew.

While being a non-political person and understanding very little of the under-currents that go on among politicians and their vested interests, I too wanted to hear more than rumors that were everyday common gossip. How true or false they were meant nothing to me. Gossips sometimes exaggerate and add tantalizing little flavors. I was never interested in politics. I didn't understand them. Somewhere deep inside me some elements of my upbringing in Saudi Arabia lingered. Call it innocence or ignorance. However I had lived long enough in Pakistan to understand something about its politics. I looked at Niazi and patiently waited for fresh information.

He shrugged his shoulders. "Everything is possible. There are no rules in this game. Who knows? There may be some hidden hands encouraging them."

"I won't be surprised if India is behind it," Shams put in, trying to prompt Niazi to elaborate. After a pause he added, "Behind it to destabilize and weaken Pakistan."

The Yugoslavs were not interested in our conversation. Occasionally they burst into laughter, so perhaps they told jokes to each other. They had nothing to do with us or we with them.

Niazi ordered a round of drinks. "Look at the Club. There's just us here. Normally it would buzz with people, with loud talking. With laughter and women chatting away. But tonight..." He sighed. "Tonight only seven of us are here perhaps witnessing the beginning of a long wait for life to turn back to normal." He paused again and went on with a tine of humor, "So long as this club lives on, let the politicians go to hell."

The lack of details disappointed Shams but just then someone else entered the bar. "Hi fellas. Things are not too good." It was our friend Mac.

"What are you saying?" Niazi asked and raised his voice.

Mac coolly waited at the bar to be served. Then he picked up his drink and joined without saying a word. Then, after looking around the room and making sure no one else was there, he began to tell us about horrific events in Dhaka. His face was grim when he said, "Bloody battles are going on between the Pakistani army and the Bengali infantry supported by locals. Thousands of Bengalis are already killed. University students and professors and it's not over. The bloodshed will continue. Only God knows for how long. As retaliation, Chittagong will have its turn tomorrow. Here there is no Pakistani army presence. Only the Bengali infantry and they, joined by locals, will attack all West Pakistanis and the Navy. There will be bloodshed." Mac took quick gulps of his drink and ordered yet another round for us.

Looking at me, he said, "Don't you think you made the right decision to send your family to West Pakistan?"

Not wanting to give details about Mac's help, I just said, "I am really thankful to the people who made their trip possible."

The conversation about the situation in Dhaka went on. After the third round of drinks, Shams and I excused ourselves and got up to leave. We had heard enough to put the fear of God into us.

"Just be careful. Stay at home tomorrow," Mac cautioned.

It was before midnight and on the way back we

passed the gentlemen with their picks and shovels. "They will probably start digging after midnight," Shams said.

There was no incident on the road and we reached home safely. My house boy Ahmad waited for my return. I reminded him that the next day was a strike and not a working day and asked him to wake me at nine in the morning.

After listening to Mac, I was now concerned about my safety and about what might happen in Chittagong the following day.

I went to bed that night thinking that I was in the thick and thin of events that would change the status of East Pakistan and that I might even witness the birth of a new nation. Recalling Mac's frightening story about the military crackdown in Dhaka. Surely I thought the army will take control, impose martial law and thus restore peace. Chittagong had only a small Pakistani military presence – mainly with its East Bengal Rifles composed of Bengalis. With these comforting thoughts I tried to sleep but, deep inside, I was uncomfortable.

The houseboy's banging hard and endlessly on the bedroom door woke me. I looked at the clock. Five minutes to seven. Either the clock had stopped, or the boy had no sense of time. I was not in a good mood when I opened the door. Before I could say a word, he spoke in a nervous tone, "Sir, come and have a look. Things are bad. The local Bengali army and the public are killing and torturing men, women and children who are not Bengalis." He paused and there were tears in his eyes. His voice trembled when he went on, "They beheaded the two Pakistani officers living below the hill."

I couldn't believe what he said. I rushed from the bedroom to the adjoining balcony and looked down at the road skirting our hillside. There were hundreds of soldiers from the East Pakistan Rifles, but I came to know later that they had rebelled and became known as Mukti Bahini, or freedom fighters. The civilians were mainly students. Together they herded non-Bengalis, such as Biharis[ii] and West Pakistanis like cattle, beating them, teasing them, and sexually assaulting the women. It was a terrifying sight. Nevertheless, as a keen photographer I rushed off to get my camera but found, to my great disappointment, that I had no film.

The two murdered Pakistani officers were our friends. Only days before, when East Pakistan was in the middle of its political wrangling and reprisals on West Pakistanis were threatened, they had comforted Rasheda and me. "There is nothing to worry about. We will protect you if the situation arises." One was a captain; the other, a second lieutenant. Both were in their twenties.

Ahmad, the houseboy, looked so frightened and nervous that the situation really began to register on me. What would happen if they came up the hill and attacked my home? I had no place to escape or hide. Then Ahmad gave me a little comfort. "They may not attack you because you work for the British Bengal Oil Company."[iii]

His words gave me some relief but then I wondered how could I trust a flaming burst of nationalism? In one moment, they could ignore every sense of right and wrong and act irrationally. They could lose their thought processes and react like mad bulls in an arena. I thought of Rasheda and my daughter Shahnaz. What if they were still here?

ENDNOTES

[i] When I say uphill, our villa was perched about one hundred and fifty feet or so above road level and had a view as far as the eye can see across the city.

[ii] The Biharis were immigrants from the Indian state of Bihar who had immigrated to East Pakistan after Independence. The Bengalis never accepted them and branded them as belonging to West Pakistan because they did not speak Bengali or try to get along with the locals. Bihar adjoins East Pakistan and is about one thousand miles from West Pakistan.

[iii] The British Bengali Company is Burmah Eastern Oil Company. A newly formed company in East Pakistan after Burmah–Shell in Pakistan sold its Shell

interests in East Pakistan to the old and well established Burmah Oil Company, its operation was mainly a storage facility for Petroleum products. As they had no marketing structure, they absorbed some of the senior staff of Burmah – Shell to manage the marketing such as the Shell inherited gas stations and other petroleum products distribution outlets. I was one of the Burmah Shell executive to be seconded. The General Manager of Burmah Shell in East Pakistan was British. He too was seconded together with a few others.

7

News about the military crackdown in Dhaka filtered down to Chittagong. Hell was let loose on the morning of March 26th when the Mukti Bahini and other locals took the law into their own hands and acted inhumanely against West Pakistanis.

Shams, my neighbor whose house was marked with a crude red X,[i] felt that they knew exactly who lived where and that the X proved it. It certainly proved something—the secession plot and the elimination of West Pakistanis from Bengal had been hatched weeks, if not months, before.

That morning, as I looked down from my bedroom window, I was truly appalled at what I saw. Shams, his wife and little son ran to my house. He puffed on his pipe as usual but the hands that held it trembled with fear. I took them to my bedroom and asked them not to leave it.

When I went outside onto the lawn, the procession of hooligans had moved on. Caught up in watching them, I didn't see two men in the white local attire and rifles in their hand walk onto my lawn. Ahmad greeted them loudly to attract my attention. They said something to him in Bengali and he replied in a soft polite voice. I walked over to them.

One spoke. "Hello, brother. Do you have anyone hiding in your house? Do you keep ammunition in it?"

I greeted them warmly and tried to make my face show only ease and innocence. "I am alone with him," I replied and pointed to Ahmad. "If you wish, please come inside and have a look."

Fortunately I didn't know at this point that Shams had sneaked out of the bedroom and watched us behind a curtain. What he felt when I offered my house for inspection can only be imagined.

"Please. Come in and have some tea with me," I went on, looking them straight in the face as I tried to project a genuine friendliness and hospitality.

"Thank you brother, we have a lot of work to do," one replied, and as they turned to go the other said to Ahmad and pointed to two cars parked outside Shams's house, "Where are the keys to those cars?"

Ahmad said something to them and they walked up to the villa on the top of the hill. A shipping executive live there but he and his family were out of the country. They were lucky. Later they found out that the house had been ransacked and left in shambles.

Perhaps I was spared because they knew I worked for a Bengali-British company. Maybe that was the reason there was no X on my house. Maybe it was the sign with my name and my company's name just outside the side. Or maybe Ahmad had reassured them when he spoke to them.

I asked him about that conversation. "Sir," he told me, "I told them that you are a foreigner who can't speak Bengali but only Arabic and English and when they asked about the cars, I said that Mr. Shams was out of the country." He smiled, walked inside, and then asked Shams who still stood behind the living room's curtain, "Sir, do you want me to make you some tea?"

Shams didn't answer, but when I walked in he exploded. "You wanted to bring those guys in here, didn't you? Are you mad? What if they had called your bluff and came in to see for themselves when you offered them tea?" He trembled in fury. His wife also reproached me angrily.

I smiled as I gave him a hug. "My dear Shams. You are not a poker player. I am and I'm good at it. I played my cards well, don't you think?" He looked back with daggered eyes as I asked Ahmad to bring us some strong tea and breakfast.

Ahmad's quick thinking and lies had saved the day.

By ten in the morning the radio continuously repeated Sheik Mujibar Rahman's declaration of independence and the formation of Bangladesh. I taped[ii] that declaration.[iii] Feeling safe inside my house, I phoned a friend of mine, a Bengali business who had a good standing in East Pakistan's political arena. To my surprise he suggested that my friends and

I go to the closest police station and take refuge there. "They will look after you and your friends. Give them my name."

That man had been close to me and my family. We'd been to his house many times. We'd listened to western and Indian classical music and live music by visiting artists together. But that day he was not the person I knew. Only a month earlier he, being a car agent, had offered me a special for a new 1971 car as he had done every time a new model arrived. In those days I seldom kept a car for more than one year so I was a steady customer. But on that day in March, he finally showed his colors. He was part of the cleansing mob! I didn't trust the offer of hospitality. It was obvious that he wanted us to step into a trap.

I wondered who I could trust. I phoned two other Bengali friends, a banker and a businessman. We met at the Club on the weekends to play poker and often enjoyed a beer or two together on Saturday afternoons when it was a men only time. We worked in the morning and most executives found it refreshing to enjoy a couple of hours at the Club after a week's hard work. Our wives never complained. They looked forward to their share of the Club later in the evening.

In less than an hour both friends arrived and suggested we just move to the main Burmah East Company compound. We chose Noor's house. He was the company's Sales Manager and my immediate boss. Shams and I knew him as a good friend and he knew my wife's family in West Pakistan. He was an icon in Chittagong's commercial community, partly because of his hospitality. I called him and explained out situation.

Without any hesitation at all he said, "You are most welcome. Leave immediately."

We wasted no time. My Bengali friends had come in a Volkswagen. We were six in all so Shams went with them while his wife and son huddled down on the back seat or floor of my car. We threw a few sheets and some empty cartons on them to give the impression that I was alone. I was told to remove my glasses and ruffle my hair. My friends wanted me to look miserable and I had no trouble showing what I felt.

I followed the Volkswagen as we came down the hill and onto the road. The Company compound was less than half a mile away and corpses littered the narrow empty road. At two places we had to drive over the massacred bodies in our hurry to reached safety.

Soon we entered the compound gate and drove uphill. At the approach to Noor's house, the road forked left to the bungalow where Rasheda, Shahnaz and I had lived for about two years before we moved out to our villa. Noor stood at the door, his arm stretched to welcome us. We hugged and embraced, then he looked at Shams, "Where are your wife and son?" Shams pointed. Noor went over to my car and semi-comically peeled off the sheets and the empty cartons. Then he helped Shams's family out.

By then it was late afternoon. Noor's wife offered to prepare lunch for us but Shams, putting his hand to his stomach said, "Hasan's cook prepared a heavy breakfast before we left." Two more cars arrived moments later, one with a common friend, Shazi, a senior businessman and the President of the Chittagong Club, and his wife and two daughters. Another couple and their child were in the other car.

We soon settled down on the veranda overlooking the large lawn. Trees formed its boundary along the edge of the hill. Beer was served. I sat and lit a cigarette as I sipped. I heard the women, almost all talking at the same time, while the men competed in a similar vocal competition. To top it all, the children's playful voices and their aimless running around almost made me forget the trauma of the day.

What are we going to do next? The danger is not over. It has just begun, I reminded myself.

My youngest uncle, who lived in the vicinity of the compound, dropped in. He was another businessman with close ties to the two Bengali friends who escorted us to Noor's house. After a beer and as they got up to leave, my uncle assured Noor and the rest of us that no one would trouble the compound. "You are a Bengali British Company and you are all safe. I will drop by tomorrow," he said and left. Our Bengali friends also assured us of our safety. They were magnificent and both were respected in the community for their contribution to the welfare of the poor and needy in Chittagong.

True to their word we were not intruded upon. However, we kept our own watch, focussing on all movements in the compound day and night. My peace was only disturbed twice. One of my Bengali colleagues, a senior member of the staff – an ex Burmah–Shell man, seconded to the newly formed Burmah Eastern Company like me – lived in this compound and came to see me the next day.

Back in 1965, when he and I were transferred from Karachi to Dhaka we shared a house with two apartments. His family had the ground floor and I the top. His daughter was six months older than Shahnaz. He was senior to me and had worked as a senior engineer for Boeing in Seattle before returning to Pakistan.

After greetings, he took me aside and came to the point, "You are living with West Pakistanis. Should the Mukti Bahini attack, you will not be spared."

"Why do you think the Mukti Bahini will attack us?" I asked.

"They know that other West Pakistanis, not just company employees, are hiding here. They will surely attack you all," he said as though doing me a favour to save me from certain death. We walked up and down the driveway, he talking most of the time.

"Come on. How do they know all this, unless..." I

paused and then went on speaking very slowly, "unless someone from the inside here reported that."

"It is better if you to live with us. It's safer...."

Before he could finish his sentence I, very politely, told him, "These people are my friends, and I am prepared to take my chances with them. Thank you any way for your concern. I will drop by later to say hello to your wife and little Shukti."

As he was leaving, he said something in a tone calculated to terrify me. "Yesterday night, they came to the compound and picked up Rashed and family. God knows what happened to them." He tramped away with a cynical expression and without the courtesy of saying good bye. Rashed was from the Punjab in West Pakistan, had been with the Company for many years and had recently been promoted as deputy to the Operations Manager. True enough. He and his family disappeared one night and were not heard of again.

I told Rashed's story to Noor and my friends. They swore at him in the filthiest words, words not available in a dictionary and therefore not suitable here.

The next day I heard more distressing news. Another colleague Shahid, a Bengali, an ex-naval officer married to a German, had joined our Company as the Operation's Manager and lived in the compound. He was a good friend and loved me like a brother. He came to the Club and reported a call from some Bengali who said that he knew that I helped West Pakistanis to hide in my friend's house and that subsequently I brought them to safety in a West Pakistani house, meaning Noor's. That person had come to his house unannounced with three others that very afternoon.

I told Shahid that his information was not true, that I had not invited anybody to join us in that house. The people in Noor's house were not West Pakistanis but originally Indians who immigrated to East Pakistan at the time of Independence in 1947. They were all Noor's friends.

While Shahid was talking to me outside, the accusers were actually in his house with the intention of dragging me out to execute me. While his wife, Helga entertained them with delicious food and drink, she had cleverly thought out a scenario for Shahid to slip out and warn me. Being German, she had seen enough of the Nazi atrocities as a child. Now as she diverted their attention, at least for a time, her alert mind worked out a strategy to get rid of them.

Finally as my friend and I were talking, we heard a sudden commotion, loud and disturbing, break out. A few compound employees started running aimlessly around the house and neighbouring bungalows yelling over and over in Bengali, "The Pakistani army is here, they will soon be here."

My friend rushed home and minutes later came back. "You should have seen those guys run for their lives when they heard that the army was here." This drama, staged by his wife, Helga, saved my life. While all this was going on and, after peace was restored, to my amazement Noor's house looked lifeless with no one to be seen.

Apparently on hearing the commotion orchestrated by Shahid's wife, they had hidden in the basement. Shahid had a great sense of humour. He knocked at the basement door, "If there are any rats in there, you can come out. The cats are away."

Shahid and his wife were popular and always was fun to have them at our parties. Soon after the war, they left Bangdalesh permanently for Germany as they could not accept the new government. Shahid was a man of principle, an ex-officer in the Pakistani Navy. He was an honorable man, loyal, and a true soldier to the oath. We kept in touch. As a marine engineer he got a job in a merchant shipping company in Germany. One day I received the sad news from his wife that he lost his life while trying to repair the boiler on his ship. It exploded. A dedicated man, he must have put his life at risk trying to do the impossible and repair the boiler. He and his wife shall always remain in our memory.

Helga's diverting news about the Pakistan army was false. It did not protect Chittagong. There was nothing, except for a small presence of the Pakistan Navy Indian Navy. I was told that the Mukti Bahini and their allies were having a ball—killing, torturing, garrotting and brutally executing men by hanging them upside down and cutting their wrists, carving out their eyes, raping women and children. Just across from our compound on the other side of the road, several persons hanging by their feet tied to the balcony railings of the second floor, screamed and tried to pull themselves up. If they had any success, trigger happy locals would open fire and kill them instantly. After the deed was done their bodies were left, their blood pouring on to the road below.

Those blood thirsty hooligans, a mob comprising of students and others who saw an opportunity to plunder, kill and abuse the weak and helpless used the lawless situation to their advantage. They were nothing but people who sometimes remain dormant but grab any possibility to commit crimes, even when there is law and order. Throughout the world there are such miscreants and little can be done to completely eliminate them from society.

The wars of independence throughout history had to be fought to achieve a goal. But why? The inevitable would come. For how long can people be kept sitting on bayonets? Why should they win their freedom by shedding blood? Both sides are hurt. Is it a law of nature or a human weakness for the oppressors to display their muscles to suppress the weak? And, during such skirmishes the miscreants avail themselves of the situation to loot and plunder. Their atrocities merge into the struggle and become part of it. A sad situation, but that is how it is all over the world when law and order weaken.

The people I met on the road to the club or those that visited my home were the activists. Their manner and behavior was gentle and respectful and there were perhaps thousands of them. I wouldn't say they were completely passive. Some may have acted otherwise. After all, a war was on. The miscreants took the situation, used it to their advantage, and gave a bad name to a just cause.

The writing on the wall was clear, but some of us didn't see it coming until it was too late. What had to happen happened. There could be no turning back.

But, *a nation was born and I was there to witness it.*

East Pakistan's burst to evolve and be born into a new entity was like all births. It came painfully, but tenderness, joy and celebrations followed. I think it is the salient hand of "nature" for billions of years which set a pattern for achieving the inevitable. And, when the time came, the inevitable took its course. The universe was born with a bang—a painful birth experienced down the line by all. In whatever situation, we have to accept the ordained, the inevitable, which is perhaps the law of nature or innate wisdom. Humans have yet to understand it.

And, in March 1971, I had yet to understand the evolution I saw, and we in Chittagong still had to vigilant.

ENDNOTES

[i] This seems to be an age-old method of discrimination. I look back to the Nazi use of yellow stars and see today the Arabic red N marks put on Christian houses by ISIS terrorists in northern Iraq.

[ii] The taping of important news, music and documentaries on history etc. is one of my hobbies and I have hundreds of such recordings.

[iii] We came to know later the announcement was by Major Ziaul Rahman from a station in Chittagong. Some years later, after the unfortunate assassination of Sheikh Mujibur Rahman staged by some ungrateful culprits who murdered the man who created a nation for his people, Zia, as he was known was himself assassinated by a Military Coup while he was President of Bangladesh.

8

For the next few days we lived with the continuous sounds of gunfire as the Mukti Bahinis[i] went on a killing spree, waging war against non-Bengali civilians while the Indian navy bombarded government installations. We were lucky to the extent that those targets were in a different part of the city but all the same we feared the day when our luck might run out.

That was the fear. The certainty was that our food supply *was* running out and we had only half a sack of rice and some lentils left. Some of the women came up with a brilliant idea and cut the lawn grass. It became a supplementary vegetable dish and tasted delicious. At least we thought so. We had no other choice.

Our other major worry was water. Noor's hilltop house depended on electrically-powered pumps, but electricity was now a thing of the past. We had an emergency and our solution was drastic. We collected all the water available in toilets and water tanks, boiled it, and locked it up in the kitchen. Everyone had a ration of just a few sips a day. The men had it easy—at least for a while. Our host's bar came alive at 6 p.m. when we were able to quench our long day's thirst with beer. But that, too, was running out.

John, a young friend, occasionally came to our rescue during this ordeal. He moved around the city with impunity, a Union Jack brandished high on his Triumph Herald. Being British, he was untouchable and the Mukti Bahini were not interested in him. Once, when he arrived with a few pounds of lamb and some vegetables, Noor's face beamed with joy. "You could not have come at a better time, John. We want you to do us a favor," he said.

"Anything you say, Noor. Just give the word."

In an almost dictatorial voice Noor said as he looked across at Shazi, the president of the Club, "The Club's bar has no use for some of the beverages there. At least it won't for a while, so why don't we make use of it? We are thirsty members who have no water to drink..."

Before Noor could finish, Shazi interrupted, "OK, I get the message but you guys have to pay for it. Nothing is free." With that, he went upstairs and came back in a few minutes with keys, a pen and a piece of paper. "Now, who will sign for what he brings?"

Noor didn't wait. "I will. I'll sign for whatever John brings. It's on me." Then he turned to John, "Pick up as much beer as you can and a few bottles of Scotch. Gin and vodka as well." As John turned to leave, he added, "And a couple of Napoleons."

John's Union Jack fluttered proudly and his wheels

churned against the asphalt I watched as he disappeared downhill and said to myself, *What magical powers that flag has!*

Luckily the phones still worked, although maybe they were monitored. Shazi called someone in the Club and instructed him to give John whatever he choose from the Club's stores. It seemed like days before we heard John's car screech to halt when he returned. We rushed out to help him unload. He had managed to visit the kitchen and had grabbed two sacks of rice, a sack of lentils and a couple of tins of cooking oil as well as our requested liquor.

John handed Shazi a piece of paper. The Club's storekeeper had written out what he'd taken and priced everything out. Shazi stepped across to Noor and became businesslike. "Please sign." Noor didn't bother to check the list. He just signed it and seconds later we all picked up whatever refreshment we wanted. Some of the women even joined in. Thanks to John it was a grand afternoon followed by excellent food.

But the next day we had a Mukti Bahini scare when several heavily armed men ran onto the lawn firing shots at targets behind them before they disappeared on the other side of the hill. Their targets emerged and fired indiscriminately in their direction before they also disappeared.

The action took less than two minutes. Most of us were lazing on the verandah at that time and, before we could realize what was happening, it was over. Silence resumed. Shams, who had been cutting grass with another guest, stood frozen with their grass cutters brandished high. The moment had been dangerous. A false move could have cost everyone their lives. But all the same, the sight of Shams holding his grass cutters high like a frozen sculptured statue was hilarious.

When they walked back to the house, no one said anything at first, but Noor had a big smile and could not control the smile developing into laughter as he looked at them, "You both looked good out there."

Shams and the other guest did not appreciate Noor's sense of humor. They were still sweating their hands shook, and their faces were still pale. They threw themselves onto a couch. There was silence for a few seconds before one of the women made a muffled noise and everyone burst out laughing. Noor disappeared and came back with two stiff Scotches for grass-cutting volunteers.

During this time the men slept in an improvised bedroom. I had never slept with so many persons in the same room since my long ago boarding school dormitory days. They were more comfortable. We slept, crammed into a twelve by twelve foot room. Some slept on chair cushions; others on the bare floor. Like boy scouts we roughed it out. I had heard snores before and had never the variety produced in that room. One man suffered from heavy breathing and huffed and puffed his way through the night. Noor's snore was classically rhythmic with an occasional loud burst of air that produced a musical tone. Someone else sounded like a goat in pain. He twisted and turned several times, limbs jerking, punching and kicking the man beside him. It reminded me of a scene from the movie *The Three Stooges* when they slept together. I always had my tape recorder ready, even when going to bed. Just in case. I made everyone listen to our night music. No one was overly amused, but I thought it fun.[ii]

A few days after that incident, we spotted a military convoy on the road below us and someone recognized Pakistani military vehicles. It was the best moment of our ordeal at Noor's house.

"Are you sure they are Pak army?" Shams asked with a tinge of uncertainty mixed with his joy.

"Yes. Very much the Pak army. It looks like they finally got through from Dhaka," someone said as we watched the long line of trucks and gun carriages stream along the road for several minutes.

"It's about time," Shams said.

We felt overjoyed and hoped that the worst was now over as we celebrated with generous quantities of beer. The women cooked more lawn grass and lentils. I was skeptical as I watched and asked myself, *Is it over? Has the army really taken control?*

Later that day and throughout the next couple of days the sound of heavy artillery and small arms fire came from different directions. We sat in suspense as the battle for Chittagong continued. Then one morning it stopped with only an occasional burst of gunfire punctuating the silence.

"It looks like the army has taken control," Shazi said. "I hope someone comes and gives us good news."

That someone was a military officer in a jeep. "Noor, are you still alive?"

Noor walked out and seconds later they embraced each other like lost friends. Major Hameed was an old buddy. They hugged, kissed, and shouted friendly abuse. "You bastards," Noor said, still hugging him. "Let me introduce you to everyone else."

"Hello, everyone. I'm glad to see my friend here alive and well. Noor, how about a drink? I can use a stiff one." After Noor handed him a drink, Major Hameed smiled and settled himself on the couch. "Ah, that was good. I haven't had one since this bloody war started."

We gathered around him like children waiting for a fairy tale. His narration of the Dhaka onslaught on March 25 was graphic and horrific as he told how they eradicated everyone they suspected of involvement in the secessionist movement. Somewhat sorrowfully he added that a great many innocent people had also been killed. "But that is war, and in war the innocent also bear the brunt." After Noor handed him another drink, he detailed his journey from Dhaka to Chittagong. "Thousands perished and we torched a lot of villages. That should teach the bastards not to break up Pakistan." He sounded proud and elated at what they had inflicted on the populace and then he went on to describe the way in which they took over Chittagong. I will never forget his words, "They ran like rats. We got their men, their women and their children. That should teach them not to fool around with the army." I just listened and shook my head in remorse.

"Noor? What happened to your hospitality?" Hameed asked, stretching out his hand with his empty glass. Noor was as stunned as the rest of us and had forgotten the courtesies of hospitality. He stared into the air, perhaps imagining those scenes of death.

After a few more drinks, the Major decided to go out to have some fun. "I'm off to burn a few Bengalis. Anyone interested in joining me?"

No one spoke. Pin drop silence filled the air. Moments before laughter and voices talking at the same time had filled the air. Major Hameed got up and walked to the door. "Don't look so grim. I was just joking. Me? Kill poor folks who don't know what the war is about? I am going to bed if you must know. I'll see you in a couple of days."

Noor was not amused. He looked at us and said in a voice that was barely above a whisper, "Though it was a joke, he shouldn't have mentioned violence in front of the women and children like that. I don't want to see him in this house again." He thought for a moment and then added, "Killing people has become a game. What would have happened a few days ago when the Mukti Bahini crossed the lawn and had decided to shoot us? The Major's joke was out of place."

During the following days, the Pakistani army secured the city and the Mukti Bahini and their accomplices disappeared from the scene—at least, temporarily. We had breathing room to think out our next move.

On April 6th the BBC announced the demise of one of my favorite composers, Igor Stravinsky. His *Rite of Spring, Petroshka* and *The Fire Bird* are among my favorite musical works. Had life been normal and I was at home, I would have played them on my recently acquired cabinet style record player and radio. The only radio I had with me was a Sanyo portable and a small tape recorder. Both ran on batteries. The tape recorder's batteries were almost dead, but the radio continued to function.

A few days passed without incidents. The office was still closed. We had some peace of mind, but did not feel free to venture outside. Finally, the all-clear signal was given. Some shops opened again and we reached out to our friends. To our dismay, many had been wiped out with their entire families. Some women and children who survived had horrible stories to tell. Some miscreants had entered their houses and decapitated or dismembered the males in front of them. Then they had thrown a coin on the bodies and told the grief-stricken audience to use it for the burials.

Stories about both sides—Pakistani, the Mukti Bahini and the miscellaneous miscreants—abounded. Without a shadow of doubt thousands of innocent people had perished and I asked myself why. Perhaps I was still being naïve. Maybe I still had the element of simplicity that I'd had as a boy I will probably never know the answer. It is not as simple as it seems. Human beings love to show their muscles, especially to the weak. Brute strength usually rules the day. Knowledge and wisdom rarely win against it.

They say that history is writer by the victors – or by those who perceive themselves to have won.

Those of us living with Noor decided to leave for West Pakistan. This was the general consensus. But how could we accomplish that? Air traffic had not been restored.

Sea passage seemed the only way. A common friend, the Naval Commodore, had left for meetings in West Pakistan just before the revolt, so our only hope was to beg for assistance from his junior officers. Noor, my boss, tried to veto my decision to leave.

"You can't," he told me. "You are the Area Sales Manager and you have work to do."

"Gladly. I would love to stay." But I had one advantage and I played it. "If you remember, Noor," I told him, "I should have been on two months leave starting from April."

"What leave? I don't remember sanctioning any leave."

"You approved my two month vacation, April 1 to May 31, in January," I reminded him, making my voice as gentle as I could. "You know why I am still here."

Noor was a wonderful boss and, as long as you performed your duties to his complete satisfaction, he was a friend. Indeed, he had proved this friendship.

"Well, in that case, you have just about two weeks left," he told me.

I responded in kind. "Whatever you say. Sir, your orders are my command."

He put his hand on my shoulder. "Hasan, I'm just joking. You go with the others and try to be back on time after two months. And, one more thing. I put you in charge of the group. Make sure they are well looked after, will you?"

"With pleasure. What about the gentlemen accompanying us? Will they have any responsibilities?"

"These old fogies need attention too," he said, referring to Shams, Shazi and the others who had shared his hospitality.

To our great disappointment passage out was not to be had. The only West Pakistani ships into port brought in troops and ammunition and they returned empty. I wondered if it was a deliberate policy to keep our "tales of horror" from reaching West Pakistan because, I later found out, things were looked on as being "normal" in our war-ravaged eastern sector. Even the radio said so. Nevertheless, we never gave up and kept pressuring friends and naval contacts to find a way out. Finally we got good news. The last supply ship due in a couple of days would carry a limited number of passengers back to West Pakistan.

We had four days to pack and leave.

We put Shams in charge of purchasing metal trunks, ropes and everything else that might be needed. Each family received a can of paint and a brush to make identification marks on our luggage. When I returned home, my loyal houseboy Ahmad waited to help me and my neighbors. At the back of my mind I had already decided not to return. As I had a gut feeling it was not yet over and might flare up again in a month or so, I packed all my personal effects—paints, decorative items, my prized record player, etc.—and gave Ahmad items like kitchen things that I felt I wouldn't need.

Everything was ready piled up for the trip to the port the following day. I took it for granted that I would be allowed to ship my car and packed the most important and valuable items in its trunk just in case there was looting. So that was where all my LP records, audio tapes, my Grundig satellite radio and spool-type tape recorder, photo albums and family documents were. The car's trunk had everything that mattered to me.

The next day a truck arrived in the early morning. After it had loaded my luggage and that of Shams, he, his family and I followed it. We entered the port about noon. Countless people milled around and the military and naval people did their best to maintain order. A young naval lieutenant waited for us at the main gate. He walked ahead, creating a path in the crowd, and we drove behind until we reached the ship's loading area. I looked up, saw the ship was named *Shams* and nudged my friend. “Do you own it?”

It was sheer coincidence but we laughed as we watched our luggage unloaded onto a large mat made of jute. As a crane lowered its giant claws onto the jute matting, several people sprang into action, grabbing giant hooks and attaching them to the matting’s four corners. When the crane began lifting, I crossed my fingers. Would the jute hold, or would it tear and drop our possessions onto the dock? Despite my worries, the luggage rose gradually and at a certain point the crane swung anti-clockwise and gently lowered its cargo into the hold below. When it shifted back with the empty mat hanging loosely, I took a sigh of relief. Our luggage was safely stored. Then a naval officer asked us to board.

I turned to him. In a soft polite voice I asked, “What about my car?”

“What car?”

“My car. It’s parked over there,” I told him and pointed it out.

“Impossible. Only passengers and luggage. Cars are simply not possible. People are even jammed into some of the storage holds. Luggage space is limited and thus restricted. I’m sorry.”

I stood helplessly. Everything I had wanted to save was lost forever.

One of our friends commented as we walked up the gangway onto the ship. “We are lucky to be on board and on our way to freedom. Forget your car. You can always get one in Karachi."

It was not the car I would miss. It was the belongings I'd packed so carefully into it. I stood at the ship's railings, sad and helpless, until I spotted a friend—the deputy manager of my bank. Suddenly I remembered I kept my wife's jewelry in a locker there. I called out to him, loudly and then louder, but with all the commotion no one could hear anyone.

As luck might have it, some of the banker's friends had also boarded and they stood next to me. They waved to him, he waved to them, and then, miraculously, he spotted me. As loudly as I could, I shouted, "The bank locker. Keep it with you." Then I used my hands and fingers to describe the box, the key and so on. Eventually he understood and signalled that all would be OK.

Meanwhile another stroke of luck happened. While I talked with the bank manager, someone in a white uniform with a few stripes on his shoulders came and stood by me. I thought he was just a naval officer.

"Well, at least you've solved your bank problem," he said.

"Thank God my friend came. I have no worries now."

"He must be a good friend to trust him with your valuables." Then he turned and looked at me. After a few seconds, as though he either recognized me or was guessing, he went on, "Are you Hasan Kabir from Government College, Lahore."

"Yes. And you?" When he told me his name I recognized him and immediately asked about his brother who had been my class mate. And so I found an old friend and, when he told me he was the ship's captain, I wasted no time. "Can you do me a favor?"

"Just ask and it will be done. What are friends for?"

I was as blunt as possible. "My car."

"What about it?"

"It is down there," I began and pointed to my car on the dock. "I put my personal important documents in its trunk. Can I get it on board?"

He thought for a few seconds and those seconds felt like an eternity. Then he put both hands on my shoulders. "Just wait a few minutes. Once that mess down there is on board and before we shut that operation down, we will somehow get your car on board. Go to the bursar and tell him I sent you. Pay him the freight charge and come back to me."

I raced off, did the financial transaction in minutes and showed the captain the receipt. He gave a few orders and someone walked up to the car. There was no fuss or display of authority. He was straight forward and seeing a hopeless situation acted sympathetically to help a friend in a time of need.

"Do you have the car keys?"

"Yes." I retrieved both the car keys and the bank locker key from my pocket and scribbled some instructions on the back of the envelope the bursar had given me – "Keep the locker key and give the man the car key." Then I wrapped both keys in a handkerchief and tied it as tight as I could.

Luckily the banker was still there communicating with his relatives. I waved to him and he waved back. "The car," I shouted, pointing to it. After a few attempts he understood what I was trying to tell him and walked up to the car. The captain took the bundle of keys from me, aimed it towards the car, and threw it. The banker caught it, read the instructions on the envelope, and soon the car was locked and on the jute mat.

I didn't want to sound ungracious, but I was worried. As casually as I could, I muttered just loud enough for the captain to hear, "I hope that mat can hold the car's weight."

"You'd be surprised," he told me. "They are triple-lined and hold up to two tons."

While we were talking, the car rose up and then was lowered into the hold. I thanked him and a few minutes later an officer came up and said something about the time of departure. The captain excused himself and added, "I will see you during our voyage." As he walked away, I looked at him and thought of my banker friend. So, there were good people left in the world after all.

It might not have seemed so in 1971 though. The birth of Bangladesh was a brutal, nasty thing with both sides, unfortunately, guilty of atrocities. It became another horrible footnote to the story of "Man's Inhumanity to Man."

I was lucky and on this note I want to say something. Was it coincidence, a hidden hand that comes unannounced to the one in need? My banker appeared from nowhere and the captain of the ship just happened to be a college colleague. *Who was helping me?* Is there possibly an element in everyone one of us that activates a kind of latent cry for help in the subconscious?

Or?

I felt it was much more than coincidence. It felt as though it was ordained. But, by whom? I don't want to go into the philosophy of what happened. The only thing I said to myself that day as I walked into the corridors to look for my friends was, "This is my lucky day."

ENDNOTES

[i] The Bengali guerrilla and armed resistance forces were known as the Mukti Bahini during the Bangladesh Liberation War of 1971.

[ii] By the way, I still have that recording in case anyone wants to hear it.

9

An hour later we felt the ship move from the dock. I rushed out of the cabin I shared with Shams and stood at the railing to watch the tugboat pull us out into the middle of the river. When its job was done, the tug gave a noisy hoot. Our ship's response was much louder—as though all of us on board said goodbye to a place we once called home.

The ship made few ripples as it set off along the Karnaphully gradually passing the Burmah Eastern's oil storage tanks and then the staff residential colonial styled bungalows with their red slanting roofs. My family had stayed in one when we first arrived in Chittagong and I wanted to tell someone, "Here I am, just three hundred feet from that home." Memories of that one and a half year stay flashed by as we moved toward the Bay of Bengal.

There had been good and bad times. East Pakistan was a new environment. The Burmah Oil Company set-up was different in the sense that everything, like work and relationships, centered around the company and the lack of external influences made its employees evolve into a tribe of their own psyche, so to speak. Although it was so self-contained, it was also possible to be happy.

For most, visits to Kolkata, Bengal (previously Calcutta and just across the border) were refreshing vacations. Kolkata had a rich heritage and offered fashionable shops, countless cinemas, theaters and concerts. I spent hours in its famous Botanical Gardens and the grand Victoria Museum. There was no huge cultural adjustment between Chittagong and Kolkata. We shared the same language and way of life. Bengal had been one of the Indian provinces split into East and West after Independence with the east part becoming East Pakistan. Now, of course, it is Bangladesh.

Chittagong though had seemed so different when we had first moved from West Pakistan. It was a city where it was possible to believe that time had stood still. The people went about their business and lived according to rules about social order set down by their ancestors. At first we found the city dull when compared to Karachi, Lahore, Islamabad and Dhaka. There were no cinemas with the latest movies or theaters, art galleries, children's parks or grand restaurants—at least in the mid-1960s.

People in West Pakistan had been more open to the outside world with a more vibrant and broader outlook. At first the whole set up seemed so uninviting, but as time went by, Rasheda and I accepted the new environment and before long we had made many friends and become a proud part of Chittagong. But we had to make several adjustments.

One Christmas Eve afternoon, one of our petroleum dealers arrived at my house with a large hamper filled with a variety of wine and liquor bottles and with a "Merry Christmas and a Happy New Year" card attached to one of the handles. Three other hampers from other dealers arrived within the hour.

I was confused. Why should these lavish gifts be showered on me? So I asked them, "What is this for?"

"Gift for Christmas and New Year," they told me. I had never been blessed with such gratitude for doing my job, especially from dealers and agents. After I thanked them for their kind gestures of appreciation, I asked them to take the hampers away. "I am sorry. I cannot possibly accept such gifts. I appreciate your good intentions..."

Before I could finish they interrupted me, "Sir, this is a customary token of our appreciation. All the other senior people in the company accept such gifts. We do it every year," one of them told ne in rather broken English.

"Well, while this might be the custom here, I am not interested." And after a pause I added, "If you want to please me, next time I visit your place, just offer me a good lunch."

They looked surprised and continued to insisted until I finally persuaded them to take their baskets away without hurting their feelings. Later I understood this this was a tradition that went back to colonial times and I realized that the lifestyle within the Burmah Oil Company vis-a vis their agents and dealers was unnatural to me and others who had served with Burmah-Shell Pakistan. The hampers had been offered in good faith because of a tradition and were not bribes as I had suspected. They probably thought I had a long way to go before I knew how to be a boss in their culture.

As time passed, the "spirit" of Chittagtong whispered, "Love me." It was quite magical. I loved the people and their ways. The environment played a role although if misunderstood it could have had adverse effects. My wife and I happily embraced our new way of life and became part of it. We were incredibly happy and life could not have been better than it was during those seven years in Chittagong.

There were a few bad experiences though. The first happened while we lived in one of the stately bungalows overlooking the Karnaphully. One morning the sky suddenly turned grey with unruly clouds and mere minutes later it seemed like night brightened occasionally by intricate streaks of lightning. Thunderous blasts made it seem like Vulcan was having a ball. I stood on the top verandah enjoying nature's theatrical show with the wind turning into a cyclone. The Karnaphully churned into violent wave swells and spilt onto the road between me and the river. As the wind's ferocity increased, the river poured its waters onto the road and our compound. Within minutes the grounds were a massive mass of water while countless fingers of lightning danced with deafening bursts of thunder.

While nature's orchestra performed, a silent and more devastating horror approached us from behind. By chance I stepped onto the toilet on the upper floor. It had a view of the airport, half a mile away and from there a massive wall of water, several feet high, advanced towards us. I had never seen anything like it before. Immediately I asked myself how could I possibly stop this destructive force entering the house.

I rushed downstairs and began collecting whatever towels, rags and such to block the bottoms of the doors and windows. While that wall of water pounded us ferociously, Rasheda, the governess, the maid and I rushed around the bottom floor collecting carpets, books and other easily portable items and took them to the upper floor. But despite my best efforts, the wall of water struck without mercy. Water seeped into the kitchen, dining and living rooms. In less than half an hour, the entire floor was three feet under water and along with it came unwelcome guests such as large lizards at least nine inches long. While they played happily in the water, I surrendered and went upstairs.

The cyclone lasted for several hours and was over by late afternoon when the water began to recede. I opened all the doors to let it find it way out, but it still took several hours. I had forgotten about my car. In waist-deep water, I half-floated, half walked my way to the garage behind the bungalow. The car was a sorry sight as it floated almost at roof level. Again I could do nothing but wait until the water receded.

The next day was bright and shiny as though nothing had happened and we began the herculean task of cleaning up. The company's maintenance team did an excellent job and the car was taken to the workshop. Two days later I found it parked outside my front door in mint condition.

For me, the cyclone was experienced in a sheltered home with some inconveniences. We went to see a cargo ship standing upright in the middle of a paddy field some few hundred yards from shore and looking like the proverbial fish out of water. It was an amazing sight that awed onlookers.

But what about the millions who lived in thatched or mud houses? What about their livestock? Their tiny cultivated patches of paddy? The loss of life and property was astronomical. Nature has no calling card. It comes and goes at its own will and in its own time sometimes leaving human misery and suffering behind and one might think that once in a lifetime is enough.

But Friday, November 12, 1971 was also a night to remember as another, and a fiercer, cyclone smashed down on us.

There had been warnings. Earlier in the morning we were warned that the approaching storm could be a level 9 cyclone. But a week earlier, I'd had a dream in which I read a newspaper's headlines saying "500,000 people perish in cyclone.' Rasheda told me, "This is one of your fictional presumptions. No cyclone can kill so many people."

"I hope so. Anyway, it was just a dream," I reassured her with a shrug and thought that she had an uncanny felling that maybe I was right. Several times I've had a dream or a feeling that this or that might happen and, amazingly, more than 90% of my premonitions have been right.

But on that night in November 1971, we were at the Club watching a movie with some friends. A strong wind lashed the city but we didn't feel alarmed. We had become so used to nature's exhibitions that we felt immune to anxiety or terror. We had heavy downpours several times a year accompanied by flashes of lightning and rumblings of thunder. These always reminded me of Beethoven's Sixth Symphony, *The Pastoral*. We were warned that this storm would be different but in our smugness we were like the boy in the Cry Wolf story and thought nothing of it.

At eight that evening someone came to the cinema hall and paged me and my colleagues to help with safety measures in the tanks storage area. We might be able to make the tanks secure but nothing could be done to the coasters or barges. They were as secure as we could make them but they bounced in the river like little toys in a bath tub.

I got home a couple of hours later with the cyclone growing stronger and more unruly. The trees on our lawn bent low. Some leaves burnt due to the friction and our daughter's doll house lifted into the air and disappeared into the darkness. The wind had no mercy. Anything not firmly rooted in the ground blew away. Luckily it began to rain and it felt like giant buckets of water were being poured on us. As the cyclone matured, no one could do anything. It seemed unending and continued to last at the entire southern coast without pity.

A couple of days later the radio estimated that about 300,000 people died but the newspaper's headline read: 500,000 Perished in Cyclone!

From time immemorial it is the same story. To be thick-skinned is one thing, but to be naïve about not taking preventative measures to relocate a massive section of the populace to safer grounds is criminal. Politicians everywhere and of every political stripe should concern themselves with public safety as they are the guardians of the nation. But I should talk. I, too, had heard warnings about the cyclone's severity and had also been blasé about them.

The second bad experience we had in Chittagong concerned my wife's sudden appendicitis attack. Under normal conditions it could have been analyzed and treated and she would have been back to normal in a few days. But that supposes that doctors are professionally trained and have an up to date medical database. What we had were quacks with no degrees worth the name even though they were employed by the Burmah Oil Company. Why didn't management question their medical competence? Why did employees take the company-provided medical care on faith? Many "whys" but really no answers.

The Burmah Oil Company was basically a storage facility for petroleum products and its clients were international oil companies such as Burmah Shell, Esso and Caltex which operated in East Pakistan and run by a handful of senior expatriates and a junior supervisory and labor staff. Perhaps local medical care was deemed a low priority. The expats had the option of being treated in West Pakistan or the United Kingdom. The "juniors" (although highly qualified) had no such options and had to entrust their lives to incompetent "doctors" whose expertise extended really to coughs and colds, minor bruises and knife cuts that needed antiseptics and bandages.

In 1967 I worked at this environment and we lived in one of those magnificent bungalows overlooking the Karnaphully when tragedy struck.

Rasheda and I were watching a film when she felt sick suddenly. Vomiting and severe stomach pains followed. As I was smoking a cigar, I wondered if it could be a reaction to its smoke. Throughout the night her pains persisted. We tried to give her soup but her system rejected it. We called the company doctor the next day. His diagnosed gastroenteritis, prescribed some medicines, but twenty-four hours later the problem had only grown worse. He made several visits and even called in the company's senior doctor, a Brit who had lived in Chittagong for many years, but this ex-pat made the same diagnosis. Four days passed and Rasheda's condition grew worse and worse.

When I realized there were no signs of improvement, I called my wife's brother in Lahore, West Pakistan, a Fellow of the Royal College of Surgeons in the United Kingdom, and explained Rasheda's symptoms. He diagnosed her problem right away as an appendix attack and took the first available flight to Chittagong via Dhaka.

Within minutes of his arrival, he confirmed his diagnosis of a burst appendix and we decided to send her to Lahore. We flew her to Dhaka where my uncle arranged everything so that she was put on a connecting flight to Lahore the same day. In pain and near death, she was lifted onto the plane by a hydraulic lift. At Lahore a medical team met us and sent her straight to hospital and her appendix was finally dealt with ten days after she had complained of pain back in Chittagong.

Later that evening my wife's brother phoned and said he had the situation under control, but prudently didn't tell me that it was still critical. I took Shahnaz, then two years old, for a stroll in the compound that evening and explained to her that Mummy had to go away to get well but would be come back soon.

As I walked with my daughter something overwhelmed me and I felt a kind of "power" that I can't describe. At first it was like a hollow feeling where everything felt faint and out of focus. Sounds and voices vanished. It was like being in a timeless void. I remember saying loud, "Let her be all right. Cure her," but I was never certain if I said those words aloud or not. I felt Shahnaz tugging at my hand and calling

"Daddy, Daddy" several times and the Nanny said something about dinner time. I still felt half awake and half asleep when she convinced to go back to the house and eat dinner. I have no explanation for what happened to me during those few moments.

The elderly, extremely immaculate nanny was a Buddhist. East Pakistan had a small population of Buddhists and as they were known to be excellent cooks and extremely clean most people employed them as cooks, houseboys or nannies. Therefore, it cannot surprise that for the two months of Rasheda's absence, she looked after Shahnaz like she was her own daughter.

At the time I was not told how close I came to losing Rasheda. It took three days just to stabilize her sufficiently so that she could undergo a massive, yet delicate, operation with only a small chance of it being successful. Her brother, together with an American surgeon, operated for four hours and she was kept under constant supervision for the next few days.

The fact that she survived was a miracle and it took her two months to recover. The American doctor also called it a miracle. Most people with a burst appendix lived only two or three days without treatment. Rasheda managed to survive for thirteen days.

It was miraculous, but it should not have happened. When I took her case to the General Manager, a Brit and colleague from Burmah Shell, but he was completely unhelpful and tried to wriggle out from any responsibility. This is when I began to judge people. Sometimes they were all smiles in good times and villainous they their faults and irresponsibility were exposed. Had the case been in the United Kingdom, for example, and come to the attention of the authorities, they would not only have suspended the licences of the doctors concerned but the Company would have dismissed its general manager. In addition, financial compensation would have been awarded to the patient. But that would have been so in the United Kingdom. It was not so in East Pakistan.

There is one more event from my years in Chittagong before I end this segment of my story. Our compound was about five miles from the city and near the harbor and mouth of the Karnaphully. One weekend, driving home at about two a.m. from the Club, the roads were empty. Then, out of nowhere, a person dressed in shabby clothes with a chalk-white face appeared in the middle of the road not more than twenty feet away. I braked hard and steered so that I wouldn't hit him but he stood unmoving, right in front of the car.

Suddenly with an antic display of hands he leaped into the air and like a missile targeted the car's windshield and went through it like smoke or like you see in the movies when spirits walk through walls. Rasheda and I both saw him go through the windshield, through the car, and out the other side. When we looked back, we saw nothing. Was it a ghost? Whatever it was, it was not of this world. His face was not like an ordinary human's. It was just like those you see in the mirror that produce distorted images and, for sure, we didn't hear a bump or any sound of hitting or running over something. The "person" that went through the car was like a beam of light and was definitely something to think about.

All this being said, the good times in Chittagong were exactly that. We had good friends, grand facilities for the senior executives and, best of all, I enjoyed my work and those who worked under me as well as my senior colleagues. It felt like being on a holiday. I could not have asked for more and I felt sad leaving it.

STEPPING INTO THE WORLD

10

I stood on deck as the ship gently ploughed the Karnaphully waters watching the row of double storeyed bungalows drift away. My last glimpse was of the one in which we'd experienced both the cyclone and my wife's appendicitis ordeal. But shortly the compound disappeared, then the last tip of land also vanished, and with that, my life in Chittagong came to an end. When we entered the Bay of Bengal I headed to meet the gang travelling with me.

The journey to Karachi was via Ceylon (now Sri Lanka). Indian Air Force planes flew over us in threatening dives twice. This bullying, although it caused a great commotion, was harmless. We were in international waters and they could do no harm. This didn't stop one of our companions' wives becoming hysterical or others spreading rumors that Bengalis on the ship would take it over. I thought we had left such fear-mongering behind.

In the case of the wife, someone took her away and I could hear him explain, "If there are Bengalis on this ship and want to get away, as we ourselves are doing, what is your problem with that? They are probably being hunted for being loyal Pakistanis. Remember that you came to Pakistan as an immigrant from India because you believed in it. Bengalis are not immigrants, though and I want to remind you that the Bengali Muslim League initiated the concept of a Muslim nation as visualized by Alama Iqbal."

He sounded very emotional and he paused to catch his breath. "I am not going to give you a history lesson, but just remember, they were the forerunners for the creation of Pakistan." He paused again and looked hard at her face, locking her eyes with his. "My dear lady, the East Pakistanis should have called themselves Pakistan rather than Bangladesh." He turned and then added, "Obviously you haven't the slightest idea of what I am talking about. You are an illiterate old woman who knows nothing of the world around you. Just keep your mouth shut."

There were only a few of us around but we were as silent as the woman for the man who had just denounced her so harshly and publicly was her husband.

The rest of the trip was uneventful and soon we were in the Karachi harbor. I stood at the railing and looked down at the docks. The yard wasn't too crowded. There were only two cars and two people standing beside them. One I recognized. Abib, was our friend. He had been the general manager of a tea company in

Chittagong for several years until he recently transferred back to Karachi.

The scene below suddenly took me back many years and a feeling of Déjà vu came over me. "Yes, I was here before," I said to myself and my mind transported me back to the day when my parents and I arrived in Karachi one early morning after my father had completed his diplomatic tenure in Saudi Arabia in 1949. I had stood with my father and when I looked down I saw a black car with two gentlemen standing next to it. They waved to my father and he waved back. That was our greeting party. I was about eleven then and it was my first time in Pakistan.

A voice from behind snapped me away from 1949 and back to 1971: "Get ready to disembark." We collected what we had and walked down the gangplank. Luggage poured out of the holds, and a truck came and loaded our items. I patiently waited for my car and as it descended onto the dock I felt like a loved one had come home. It was a joyful moment. I not only had my car but all my cherished valuables.

Customs began clearing our luggage and everything seemed just perfect until an officer asked me to pay import duty and tax.

"Tax and import duty on what?"

"You are bringing a car from outside," he said in broken English.

"What do you mean outside?"

"You are importing a car."

I looked at him. “Sir, I am not importing a car. I am bringing a car from one province of Pakistan to another province of Pakistan. It’s just like driving a car from Lahore, Punjab to Karachi in Sind. Do you impose import duty on that?”

“No. You brought a car from outside,” he kept repeating.

Before he could finish his next repetition, I cut him off. “Are you saying that East Pakistan is ‘outside’? Is it not one of the provinces of Pakistan?”

“Yes. But…but…” He kept repeating himself over and over perhaps because he didn’t know the answer to my questions.

I raised my hand with the palm open to shut him off before he could say anything more. I was argumentative and hard. He deserved it though. He kept referring to East Pakistan as though it was another country. That attitude that created the rift and misunderstanding between the peoples in the two wings of Pakistan and politicians can answer for that. But, I knew I had to change my strategy.

I was polite. “Excuse me, sir. Do you know what is happening in East Pakistan?”

He looked confused. Apparently he had no clue. The local radio stations had not reported the true nature of the secession, and the government had kept the truth from the public. As the customs officer was oblivious, I decided not to enlighten him. It would complicate matters and give him more reason to levy duties and taxes. I had to think quickly.

Seeing no way of changing his mind and with my friends waiting for me, I decided to pay the 10,000 rupees he requested. He took the money, scribbled something illegible on a sheet of paper, and I drove my car out to my friend Abid's house following the luggage truck. From there I called Rasheda and told her what had happened. She thought I was joking. People in West Pakistan didn't know anything about the tragic events. After talking to her for some time, I called her uncle in Karachi and within an hour I was in his house.

After a good hot cup of tea, I reflected. The ordeal was over. I would never go back to East Pakistan – or Bangladesh. I had decided that the moment I'd stepped onto the ship at Chittagong. As well, I'd mentally resigned from my job. However, I could not be unthankful. The Chittagong experience had given me great happiness.

But what about morning of March 26th when men, women and children were assaulted and abused. That had been the beginning of the end for me. I had seen too much and, no matter what reasons or justification was offered, I would never be used to that kind of political violence. I am what I am. While that might be interpreted in many ways, for me it meant *no violence on innocent people whatever the cause. Period.*

Soon my wife and daughter joined me in Karachi and enjoyed the hospitality of her uncle for several months before we moved back to her parents in Lahore. During that time in Karachi, the situation in East Pakistan was not settled until after a war with India, Pakistan surrendered title and Bangladesh became an official nation.

Strangely, the war even followed me to West Pakistan. The whining of a bomb put shivers into us one afternoon. We rushed to take shelter and I picked up Shahnaz and lay of top of her. The bomb, dropped by an Indian pilot escaping the Pakistan Air Force, exploded onto a house just fifty feet away. Splinters riddled the concrete of our house and the windows shattered and fell in. luckily we had stacked sandbags around the house and thus escaped a major catastrophe.

I conclude this part of my story with a reflection on the value of friends beginning with Mac's alert to send my family to West Pakistan and the generosity of the gift of airline tickets. I say gift because, a year or so later when I had moved to Saudi Arabia, I asked him to tell me the entire amount I owed him. He refused payment. The tickets had been a gift. Mac had also invited me to join the Freemasons and by the time I left Chittagong, I was a Master Mason.

MY PERSONAL ROLL OF HONOR:

- *Rafi* who accompanied my wife by train to Dhaka to catch her flight to West Pakistan on March 11, a mere fourteen days away from the secession of East Pakistan.

- I'm grateful to *the two Bengali friends* who risked their lives to escort Shams, his family and me to Noor's house.
- And of course *the banker* friend who took custody of the key to the locker containing my wife's jewelry at the Chittagong port.
- *Noor*'s hospitality knew no bounds. He and his wife were marvelous to all who shared their home during the worst and most tense period of our lives. They made us feel that we were one family.
- *John*, who replenished our stock of alcoholic beverages from the Chittagong Club.
- *The ship's captain* who saved my car.
- *Abib* who met us at the Karachi port with transportation and an invitation to come home with him for those who had no other place to go.
- *Khalajan*, my wife's aunt, with whom we stayed for months and who treated us with love and affection.
- I will never cease to be thankful for my loyal houseboy, *Ahmad* for his tactful handling of the Mukti Bahini when they visited my home the morning of the 26th of March, 1970. His quick thinking saved the day and almost certainly my life.

- And, of course, *Helga* for her quick thinking that averted tragedy.

In retrospect those uncertain days were a frightening experience. No one knew the outcome. We lived with the thought of someone coming in and emptying his machine gun on us. I was safe and sound, but my thoughts were with those who didn't escape. Our ship was the first and last passenger ship to leave Chittagong for some time.

Full scale war between India and Pakistan started at both fronts in the east and west. The Indians joined hands with the Bengali secessionist army. A few days after the surrender of the Pakistani army in December 1970, life returned to normal in Chittagong. One afternoon I got a call from a banker friend in Karachi saying that he had something for me. Being a banker he had traveled to Bangladesh on business and while in Chittagong he happened to meet the friend I had given the locker key to. He then gave my Karachi friend Rasheda's jewelry box to deliver to me.

The box was scotch taped and sealed. Just as I had left it in the locker—unopened, safe and sound. Unbelievable, but true. Another surprise was the same Karachi banker meeting the Finance Manager of Burmah Eastern Company, a Bengali. This man was my colleague and good friend who knew that I wouldn't be returning and sent some money that I was due through the banker. Another good deed by another trusted friend.

Who says there are no true friends in this world? A true friend is one who walks in when others walk out. My Chittagong experience proved this to me. But while I was understanding this, I kept thinking: This part of my life has ended. What is next?

11

A few months after I returned to West Pakistan after leaving East Pakistan I met a Kuwaiti gentleman who convinced me to go to Kuwait with him where he would get me a good job with the Kuwaiti National Petroleum Company. I agreed and true to his word he took me to meet a gentleman in the Ministry of Finance. Seeing my qualifications, he made me fill a form. I, who have a good knowledge of Arabic, filled it giving all what was required – in Arabic.

Meanwhile to my good luck I came across the Regional General Manager of Pakistan International Airlines in Kuwait. Ejaz Ahmad was with me at college in Lahore and he insisted that I stay with him and leave the hotel. His one old son was so loveable that I used to take him out to the seaside across from their apartment. He was so cute that I nicknamed him Buju Buju. Today he is successful businessman in Dubai. His older son has become a popular singer and has an orchestra that is well known in the subcontinent and abroad. His name is Salman and that of his musical group — *Junoon*.

Two weeks later I got the job with the Kuwaiti Oil Company.

Kuwait had changed since my last visit in 1958, when I was driven across the desert from Basra in an official car arranged by my father just after the Military Coup in Iraq to catch a flight to Karachi. How I remember that journey across the desert in August with the temperature exceeding 120 degrees and with hundreds of men, women and children fleeing the military regime in Iraq and dotting the landscape. Now the city was well planned with asphalted roads, high rise buildings and modern residential areas. I hadn't quite expected that because I had expected the traditional Arab style houses of the 50s.

My boss a Kuwaiti was very pleasant and my first assignment was to survey all their gas station outlets. The report I gave was not encouraging. The locations and set up of the gas stations did not comply with international rules of safety. He was impressed and soon appointed me as Marketing Assistant to him. Salary was good, the housing also and then were some perks. This was too good to last. Two months later, he called me to his office. "You are not an Arab. You are a Pakistani."

"Yes" I replied, a bit confused.

"This job is for a Kuwaiti, and if no Kuwaiti, an Arab."

"But you must have known that I was not an Arab from my application."

"I did not read it I just gave you the job because you spoke Arabic like an Arab and have the experience of working with an international oil company. There was no need to read your application. Yesterday one of my assistants in the Staff Department brought in your application form and read out the section where you have put your nationality. Anyhow, I don't want to lose you. I can help you."

He scribbled something on a piece of paper and handed it to me, then picked another piece of paper and wrote something and signed it. I read the first one which had the name of someone and an address with a telephone number. The second paper was addressed to the same person, it just said, "Please help him. He needs your assistance."

"This person is a good friend. He will help you to get an Arab passport," he told me and I will not mention here the nationality of the man or what Arab passport he referred to. "Oh yes," he added, "If you come to an understanding, his fee is 500 Kuwait Dinars.

The idea didn't appeal to me or to my friend Ejaz.

After some time looking at other options, Ejaz said, "Good jobs like the one you have are hard to get. You have a future here and, after all, you can always keep your Pakistani Passport. Think about it"

I couldn't get myself to accept the change of citizenship. On top of that was the fact of getting it through a "back door" arrangement, even through an embassy. It was not and is not my style.

The next day I politely refused the offer and thanked him for his concern. He was genuinely sorry to let me go. I decided to return to Pakistan but first I wanted to visit my mother in Saudi Arabia. I had not seen her since she and my father left in 1966 and as I was in the vicinity decided to visit her before returning home.

On the aircraft seated next to me was a gentleman who during the flight had conversations on a number topics including the prospects of job openings in Saudi Arabia as it was on the verge of a financial boom. He suggested that I look for something before returning to Pakistan, mentioning that he knew of a possible position. The Embassy of the United States was reorganizing their Commercial Section and he offered to assist should I needed his help.

Hearing all that, I remembered once my father writing to me in 1968 to join him in Jeddah and he would help me to get a better job there in the oil industry through some of his old friends. At that point I was not interested. There was no job anywhere better than where I was.

Destiny has its own ways of "giving," and I was led by its hands to find a new home in Saudi Arabia.

I came to Jeddah from Kuwait on a visitor visa to spend some time with my mother and I suggested that she return to Pakistan with me. She refused. She was more at home in Saudi Arabia where she had friends and good neighbors. That was true. During my stay with her she always had friends visiting and the neighbors' daughters coming in and out doing errands for her. She had a maid that did all the house work. With all these comforts she was at peace. Yet I felt that she needed me to be with her. So I decided to stay.

One day my mother said, "Go and see your old friend from school, Wahib bin Zagar." Wahib and I had gone to the local school in Jeddah when we were kids.

"That was long ago," I said. "He wouldn't remember me."

"On the contrary. Your father met his father several times when we returned. They've been friends since the good old days. He will surely remember you."

I agreed and she told me where to go. Jeddah had not developed much since the time we left in the late 1940s albeit with a few exceptions. The city wall was not there and a few buildings were where the wall had been and within the city some new buildings were being built. I went to a part of the downtown area with narrow roads and gullies – the remnants of old Jeddah.

After asking people and shopkeepers to direct me to Wahib bin Zagar's office, someone pointed to a narrow lane. I couldn't believe my eyes. How could an office be located in there. On either side were makeshift general stores selling garments, electrical equipment and toys. The path in between was hardly three feet wide. I zigzagged between pedestrians until I found a doorway with a small name plate. I climbed several steps and entered an office with several small rooms on opposite sides.

My mother had told me to meet Wahib's father and uncle first. When I introduced myself they met me very graciously. Then I met Wahib. He too was warm and friendly. When he heard my story about East Pakistan and my professional experience working in one of the world's major oil companies, he was impressed and took no time in offering me a job. He was the agent for British Petroleum and asked me to run its sales department.

The Bin Zagar Company was also in general trading, tea, detergents, foodstuff and a host of other items as I found out when he showed me his set up. All his offices were crowded in one big hall. It had an informal atmosphere and I was not impressed. Compared to my previous status, his office was like one of my small town petroleum agents in Pakistan. But, I needed a job. I accepted his offer and the next day I was in attendance before any of his staff — even the tea boy!

He appointed an assistant to show me around and the BP workshop and their other facilities. This went on for about three weeks. I was not happy and definitely not in the right place. I wanted something more professional than going around to sell BP products to gas stations.

I rang the gentleman I had met on the flight to Jeddah and asked him if he could help me. He promised to contact someone in the U.S. Embassy to find out if they still needed someone in the Commercial Section.

The next day he called back and asked me to go to the embassy and then ask for a certain gentleman. Within minutes I was sitting with the Commercial Attaché. As it happened he had been posted in East Pakistan during the secession period and the emergence of Bangladesh. He had seen it all – the politics, the passions, the horrific violence. These events connected us and he became sympathetic.

Shortly afterwards he took me to large room and introduced me to the Ambassador of the United States. He was extremely friendly and in minutes we were talking about their future plans to expand the Commercial Section's activities. Then His Excellency suddenly said, "How good is your Arabic?"

I explained my background to him and that my mother was an Arab from Saudi Arabia. Suddenly he said something in Arabic. I recognized his Arabic. He spoke with an Iraqi accent. Having spent time in Iraq when my father was posted there I was able to reply him in that dialect. He was impressed and picked up the telephone and said something in a whisper. Soon a gentleman walked in and sat next to me. The ambassador said to him, "Can you tell me which part of the Arabic world Mr. Kabir comes from?"

Judging from his accent, the man was a Palestinian. I replied in Hejazi (i.e. Saudi style) and we conversed on different topics. The Ambassador interrupted, "Tell me, how is his Arabic and where does he come from?"

The man grinned, "Your Excellency are you testing my Arabic? To me Mr. Kabir is a Saudi and judging from the language he comes from Makkah area."

The Ambassador got up and shook my hand, "Congratulations, Mr. Kabir, you got the job." After a pause, he looked at the gentleman who had tested me, "By the way, Mr. Kabir is from Pakistan. He sure fooled you." A few more pleasant words were exchanged and we left.

At the Commercial Attaché's office he briefed me about my job description. He and I got into his car and drove to the downtown area. We walked to a building in the congested part of the city, not too far from the Bin Zagar's office. We walked up a flight of stairs to the second floor. On that floor there were four apartments, on each door was a commercial sign board, one of them said, "Commercial Section of the United States Embassy."

I couldn't believe my eyes. But then those were the only available facilities where business organizations were located. The office was dark and gloomy. One gentleman got up to meet us. He was a secretary *cum* contact man with local businessmen, an Indian gentleman who later on proved a great help to me.

After we left, the attaché drove me to a more developed part of the city. We reached the Jeddah Palace Hotel. Below it were a few newly built office facilities. We entered one of them. It had a large hall with a glass wall fronting the road. There were two rooms, a kitchen and a washroom. False ceilings were studded with lights and central air conditioning vents. The rooms were freshly painted, carpeted and furnished with desks equipped with typewriters and a photocopy machine.

"This will be your office," he told me, pointing to one of the rooms. The other room was for the commercial attaché.

I knew then that I was in the right place and made the right choice. It was my kind of environment. All was good, but there was one thing I never anticipated – the Bin Zagar Company becoming a multi-million dollar organization in less than ten years. Had I stuck with them and roughed it out, I would have been somewhere in its upper management. Well, that was not to be and I had no regrets.

The next step was, to go to Beirut, Lebanon to get a crash program training at their embassy. My position was a commercial officer. That carried a lot of weight with the flow of American businessmen that began to descend into Saudi Arabia all looking for agents or representatives or joint ventures or a piece of the action in government projects. These days were the beginning of the financial boom and Saudi Arabia was building its infrastructure. My job was to get American businessmen connected.

Jeddah, Riyadh and Dammam were my regular

visiting points to sell American products. I enjoyed my job. It gave me an exposure to the senior government officials and I developed personal contacts with the top commercial elite. They were all in the process of developing into conglomerates from little businesses like Bin Zagar to organizational giants. The Saudis are business minded and in a very short time they were as good if not better than their counterparts in the western world. They learn fast.

I have many letters of appreciation from U.S. companies. I was presented with two bronze medals – one from OPIC (Overseas Private Investment Corporation) and the other for Peace and Commerce. The Gold and Silver went to senior Saudi government officials.

Having no business directory in Arabic or English, I composed one in English giving some details on each business, their owners etc. It was published in the United States. I called it *Doing Business in Saudi Arabia.*

Though I was a third country national employee, I had the respect and appreciation from both the U.S. authorities and Saudis. I served both with loyalty and sincerity. I must add here, walking on the streets of Jeddah was not much different from those I walked to school on in the old days. Some of the streets and roads were paved, most were not. The old port building was just a historic residue of the past. From the top of newly constructed high rise shopping center I looked down at the Port building and the adjacent building that had housed the old desalination plant.

My thoughts went back to the days when I accompanied my father to the port. In those days ships, passenger or cargo, anchored a few miles out at sea. No sea port in the modern sense existed then. The 1970s Jeddah was transforming from the old to the new with the oil boom just beginning to show its mark. I was lucky to be there to see such a miraculous transformation and to have had a good job.

One afternoon a Saudi gentleman came into my office as many did to look for business opportunities. After telling me a story about how he had lost all his fortune in a bad business deal, he opened his brief case and showed me a Saudi Riyal 10 note (about US$ 2.5), "That is all I have."

I felt sorry for him and almost decided to dig into my pocket and assist him with whatever I could afford. On second thought I decided against it. He might not have taken it graciously and felt insulted.

Closing his brief case he got up and shook my hand. "See if there is an American company that needs a Saudi partner. I have big contacts with government officials and ministers. I can also get government funding for big projects." Before leaving I made him fill in a visitors' form with his full contact details. I wondered as to how a person with such little money could have the high contacts that he claimed to have.

I had introduced a 'Visitors Form' to be filled by any

one coming to the Commercial Section – Americans, Saudis, Others. I wanted to know their interests and what they could offer. Almost a year later, an American businessman visited my office with an idea about decongesting the Jeddah sea port. I was not too familiar with the port's problems until he explained that ships were anchored for months two to three miles out at sea waiting to be unloaded. That was like the old days when my father was posted here, pilgrims were off loaded on to sail boats and brought ashore.

What he was looking for was a Saudi businessman with enough influence to get his proposal accepted by the Government. At first I couldn't think of anyone. There were several shipping companies and when I called a few and explained the proposal, they were, either not too enthusiastic or the owners were out of the country and no one responsible to take a decision. Suddenly I remembered the gentleman who came to see me with the Saudi Riyal 10 note in his brief case.

I went through the visitor forms and after some search found him. He had said that he had good contacts with ministers and government authorities. Now we would see. Finally the two parties met and came to an agreement. The idea was to bring in LST vessels and with a stevedoring company unload the cargo. With this operation they would unload between 500 to 800 tons a day. The idea was accepted by the minister concerned and they were in business.

I heard later on that the Saudi gentleman was *not fair*

with the American party. In my experience, this is what happens when a person with a poor background who had not seen wealth condescends to the lowest order of morality. It was not only him, but I saw it with many who today call themselves sheikhs.

To top it all these so called sheiks were immigrants who came to this country for Hajj and stayed on a few decades before. It was easy then to get the nationality. It was said that some time ago an official used to carry a basket full of "Nationality Documents" to distribute to those who wanted them. As a result the poverty stricken pilgrims who decided to stay on availed themselves of that golden opportunity. There were Indians, Yugoslavs, Russian or Central Asian, Indonesians and so on. If they were put in trousers and shirts today it would not be difficult to guess their origin. They would look like their compatriots performing the Hajj or the labor force coming from their countries of origin. So, in order to give them the Saudi look, the Arab dress became compulsory because it transformed them into looking like "sons of the soil look."I noticed the same conversion of dress in Kuwait and elsewhere in the Gulf after the financial boom to justifyor differentiate these earlier immigrants from the later imported employees. In a nutshell the dress said: "Remember, I am the master and you are the servant."

On the other hand the pure Saudi never had or has bestowed upon himself the title of Sheikh. They were just businessmen and people address them as such out of respect for the wealth they acquired as a result of the oil boom. I am also proud to say that I had helped several young Saudi boys returning from the United States after completing their studies to enter into business at a young age. Most of them have done extremely well. Some could even be bracketed with some of the richest in the world.

The reason for their jump start success was that timing is everything. Saudi Arabia was at the beginning of the oil boom and money poured down like rain. The country needed to build its infrastructure, roads, buildings, telecommunication, defense, factories and businesses with joint ventures, the import of labor and food, and the list goes on. The 1970s was something to witness because in less than a decade the country was transformed from that "medieval" disorganized kingdom to a modern nation. I am proud to have witnessed that magical accelerated growth. It was as if someone had Aladdin's lamp. Hats off to the Royals who were at the helm of affairs!

In 1976 that Saudi gentleman who got the stevedoring contract came walked into my office with a job proposal that had a good salary and benefits. I was attracted to it but was sorry to leave my employers who had done so much for me. I sent in my resignation to the Commercial Counselor of the embassy. He replied saying how sorry he was to lose me and that wished me well on my new assignment. I was appointed as

Administration Manager to look after the South Korean Stevedoring staff (about 1600), the Norwegian personnel handling the LSTs and local employees. In 1986 a prince, the King's youngest brother offered me a job as General Manager to look after the U.S.-Saudi joint venture to carry military supplies to the Kingdom and its distribution at various points. I served that company until his sudden demise when we lost the contract. His daughter took over the company but worked in different fields.

THE SAUDI GAZETTE FRIDAY MAY 26 2006

Fans pack Al-Ahli Stadium to see the first cricket exhibition match in Jeddah, Thursday – Photos by Saeed Bahmishan and Badar Al-Asmari.

CRICKET AT LAST

I must add that as a keen cricketer, while watching an international tournament in Dubai on TV, an idea struck me. Why not have similar matches in Saudi Arabia? Would they be successful? The Saudis had no concept of the game. They love football and competed internationally but there was a very large ex-patriates community of Indians, Pakistanis, Sri Lankan,

Bangladeshis, British and other cricket-playing nations perhaps totalling over one million.

Several teams played on Thursdays and Fridays (the latter being a holiday in the Arab world) on desert makeshift wickets. Occasionally there were several Arab spectators who just enjoyed the crazy expats playing all day under the burning sun where temperatures can reach up to 100 degrees Fahrenheit. Maybe Noel Coward should have added Saudi cricketers to his mad dogs and Englishmen song!

The idea matured in my mind and I went to see the Princess who was the boss of our company, knowing that as she was the niece to the King it should not have been difficult to obtain permits from local authorities (i.e. the ministry of sports) to set up cricket as an official game in the Kingdom.

I explained the prestige we would get by becoming part of the international cricket fraternity. World teams would set foot on Saudi Arabian soil when we had stadiums and official Saudi teams. And of course some earnings would come from that to maintain the facilities. The idea was too foreign to her. However, she asked me to write a letter to the Ministry explaining in detail what we wanted. She signed it and asked me to fly to Riyadh (the capital) and deliver the letter to the Minister (who was her cousin).

He met me very cordially and in no time liked the idea and asked me how to prepare the wording on the License should read and he would sign it. I flew back to Jeddah, discussed it with the Princess and showed the draft of the license then, with a covering personal letter from her, I flew to Riyadh and delivered her letter and the license written in Arabic to the Minister who promised to sign it and send it officially by post.

Within the week we received the official license. From that moment Saudi Cricket Center (SCC) was established and the Princess appointed me as the CEO and added it to my other duties.

With such a license, my next step was to apply to the International Cricket Council in London.[ii] It was not easy. They had little knowledge about cricket activity in Saudi Arabia though some in the past had tried to get membership but failed due to absence of official recognition from the host government.

The Princess and I agreed not to divulge our progress. Meanwhile I studied the ongoing activity of cricket in the Kingdom. I found expats spending their weekend afternoons playing cricket and in each town or district they formed Associations, Each Association had several teams with a chairman and office bearers. All this was unofficial because such an activity in the Kingdom could face severe punishment. Even the word "Association/s" is banned unless otherwise authorized. I found six established associations more than sixty teams. All were well established and played tournaments against each other and occasionally flew to neighbouring Arab counties to compete.

To me, the grounds were set to present my case to

the ICC in London. The game was alive in Saudi Arabia. To obtain membership would give the Saudi Cricket Center full control and officially put the Kingdom on the world Cricket map.

Finally in 2001 we obtained the ICC membership and automatically also became a member of the Asian Cricket Council (ACC). Then I invited a senior Cricketer in Jeddah and gave him the good news. He recommended another gentleman join us. We three began working out how to approach the heads of associations to join the SCC and establish the game officially.

At first it was not easy. Many asked why they, being seniors in the game, should they become subordinates to an unknown entity that suddenly emerged from nowhere. I explained that had they approached the local authorities for a license at first they might have been in control but that now they had to accept the inevitable. It took time, but finally SCC was accepted by all.

Funded by ACC and ICC they helped develop the grounds and train players. In due course we were invited to participate in International matches with affiliate countries and surprisingly won a few.

By 2006 we were bold enough to host an international event. We invited a Pakistan official XI to play the rest of Asia comprising India, Bangladesh and Sri Lanka. The expat community did not believe the news at first but as the teams arrived and stepped into the grounds, suddenly there were countless spectators, some climbing onto the walls of the stadium. (We had hired a local football stadium and converted it to a Cricket with the condition that we repair any changes after the match.) The stadium was full with nearly 14,000 spectators. Some managed to get onto rooftops of surrounding buildings. Pakistan won the three-day tournament and I was proud to hand over the winning trophy to the Pakistan Captain, Inzam ul Huq, (one of the best cricketers in the world).

With this event the SCC has established its name. Today it is on its way to compete in the next World Cup. It was not an easy "innings" for me. The Princess appointed me as Deputy Chairman with her as the Chairman. With the license I gained membership from cricket's world body – the International Cricket Council in London – and the Asian Cricket Council in Malaysia. Cricket was firmly established in the Kingdom and its team qualified to participate (subject to qualifying in competitive matches) in the World Cup in 2015.

I greatly enjoyed my life in Saudi Arabia and I felt fulfilled in so many ways with the cricket recognition as maybe a crowning achievement. However life is never predictable, thank goodness. I was born in Jeddah and no one at that time could have or would have predicted where I would spend my retirement.

ENDNOTES

[i] Father Klaver was the Principal and our maths teacher and was the one who wrote to Cambridge University to revise my failed English Language paper when I first appeared for the Overseas School Certificate in 1954.

[ii] Years later the ICC moved its headquarters to Dubai.

12

I retired in early 2012 and as I said, my wife and I have enjoyed every minute of our stay in Saudi Arabia. We made good friends, lived comfortably and had a host of other facilities that one can usually only wish for. Both our daughters went to the best foreign schools in Jeddah and subsequently to Franklin College in Lugarno, Switzerland for their higher education. But I am writing these pages happy and comfortable after settling in Canada where my daughters are.

The older one Shahnaz is married to Dr. Tahir Nizami, the son of an icon in journalism and founder of a leading Newspaper in Pakistan. His father was a close friend of the founding father of Pakistan, Mr. Mohammad Ali Jinnah and had a postage stamp was dedicated to him. We are proud to have him as our son-in-law. He, himself has become an icon. A doctor by profession, he ran his own IVF clinic and was the first doctor in Pakistan to produce a test tube baby. They moved to Canada in 2001 and got their citizenship in

2004. The photo below shows them at Lighthouse Park, one of their favorite sites.

Our second daughter Tanya, after leaving Franklin College, Lugarno joined Brunel University in England where she achieved a Master's Degree in Creative

Writing. Her interest in that field took her to Vancouver Film School, (VFS) in Vancouver B.C. in Canada where Shahnaz. After finishing her course with the VFS, she got her Canadian residency and shortly afterwards married. In 2014 she took out her Canadian citizenship.

Her husband, a Canadian of Danish origin, teaches in the VFS where they met. He too is an icon in his field. In the last four years he has earned "best instructor of the year" awards. That is only the beginning for him. Now our daughter is also employed by the VFS in administration.

My wife and I are the happiest parents to have such

daughters and sons-in law. Now it is our turn to find a place to sit and look back at the years gone by when we were beginning our lives. After my mother passed away at the age of 92 on January 19, 2011, I lost interest in staying in Saudi Arabia. As far as my maternal relatives are concerned, they don't exist for me after their unjust treatment and attitude all those years ago towards my parents.

As for Pakistan and Bangladesh, all my uncles have passed away. Most of my cousins have moved on to different parts of the globe – England, the United States, Australia and New Zealand and India. My sister Latifa, heer husband Salim and family have been well settled in the United Kingdom for many years. Her daughter, a barrister, has just become a Queen's Counsel (or Q.C.). We are proud of her.

Canada, where Shahnaz and Tanya settled, is a perfect choice for Rasheda and me to spend our golden years near with them. As for my Rasheda, she too had lost her aged mother (on November 7, 2009). She has eight brothers and sisters who are all married and enjoying a very comfortable life in Pakistan. She was very attached to her mother and with her passing away she also felt that our move to Canada was the perfect choice. We arrived on the 15th of March 2013.

Living in Saudi Arabia was a great experience. I had seen it as a child in its medieval state with limited modern amenities and later watched the magical transformation of its infrastructure that very few nations can boast of. That was an enviable experience. I have enjoyed working with all levels of people, whether employees or colleagues. As they say all fingers are not the same. I have had bad experiences not expected from certain classes of people, especially from those I had helped to develop their commercial successes from literally nothing to something but that's, as they say, the way the ball bounces.

There is something I have learnt working with various people. Some from the outside are friendly but hold a dagger behind their backs. If any of those people are reading these lines they very well know whom I am referring to. Their religious theatrical displays are only a façade. Let me leave it at that.

I have completed all that I remember about my life for my children and grandchildren to read about the "good old days" my wife and I have had. May they write their own equally fascinating stories.

My final advice, *never give up.* I once saw an ant climb a wall and at some stage fall to the ground. It went back to the wall and up it went. It fell again and again but it continued until, finally, it reached the top and disappeared to where it wanted to go.

Be that ant!

THE END?

MY LATEST PASTIME -- OR MY DOODLES

ABOUT THE PUBLISHER

WESBROOK BAY BOOKS is a new Vancouver-based company specializing in publishing top-quality fiction. Visit our website — www.wesbrookbay.com — and buy our books from its store.

Beverley Boissery —

*The Convict's Thumbprint; tHAD (*Books 1 and 2 of the Wahmurra series)

Forgotten Secrets (2015); *Theo Bentley's War of 1812* (2014)

WP Gatley —

*The Apostle's Apprentice (*forthcoming)

Kelsey Greye —

All That Remains (2014); *A Bitter Root* (2016)

Mark Hadley —

The Red City (2015); *The Black Sword* (2016)

Jono Howard –
A Sweet Story (2015)

Hasan Kabir –
Journey to Life (2015); *The Medallion* (2016)

BA Schellenberg –
A Prince Among Dragons (2015)

Jack A. Taylor –
The Cross Maker (2015); sequel forthcoming

Special thanks to:

Everyone who encouraged me – friends both new and old.

And to Katie Drysdale of Tapestry. I appreciate your proof reading help.

Hasan

Special thanks to: